# The Human Journalist

# The Human Journalist

*Reporters, Perspectives, and Emotions*

JIM WILLIS

Afterword by Col. Ann Norwood, M.D., Mary
Walsh, and Penny Owen

Westport, Connecticut
London

**Library of Congress Cataloging-in-Publication Data**

Willis, Jim, 1946 Mar. 19–
    The human journalist : reporters, perspectives, and emotions / Jim Willis ;
afterword by Ann Norwood, Mary Walsh, and Penny Owen.
       p. cm.
    Includes bibliographical references and index.
    ISBN 0–275–97283–6—ISBN 0–275–97307–7 (pbk. : alk. paper)
    1. Journalism—Psychological aspects. 2. Journalism—Objectivity. 3. Journalistic ethics.
I. Title.
PN4771. W55   2003
070.4'01'9—dc21     2003053566

British Library Cataloguing in Publication Data is available.

Library of Congress Catalog Card Number: 2003053566
ISBN: 0–275–97283–6
     0–275–97307–7 (pbk.)

First published in 2003

Praeger Publishers, 88 Post Road West, Westport, CT 06881
An imprint of Greenwood Publishing Group, Inc.
www.praeger.com

Printed in the United States of America

The paper used in this book complies with the
Permanent Paper Standard issued by the National
Information Standards Organization (Z39.48–1984).

10  9  8  7  6  5  4  3  2  1

**Copyright Acknowledgments**

The author and publisher gratefully acknowledge permission for use of the following sources:

Extracts from *Intimate Journalism* by Walt Harrington, published in 1997 by Sage, reprinted with permission.

Extracts from Scott Maier, "Getting it Right? Not in 59 Percent of Stories," *Newspaper Research Journal*, Winter 2002, Vol. 23, No. 1, pg. 10, reprinted with permission.

Extracts from Christine Urban, "Examining Our Credibility," *American Society of Newspaper Editors*, reprinted with permission.

Extracts from Jim Willis, "Journalists Heal Wounds During Bombing," *The Edmund Sun*, April 19, 1998, pg. 5, reprinted with permission.

Extracts from *The Daily Oklahoman*, "Fall of the Wall Saluted," by Jim Willis, November 10, 1999, pg. 1.

Extracts from a conversation on Feb. 25, 2002, with Ann Norwood and Mary Walsh concerning coverage of international events.

Extracts from a conversation on Feb. 28, 2002, with Ann Norwood and Mary Walsh concerning coverage of 9/11 tragedy.

Every reasonable effort has been made to trace the owners of copyright materials in this book, but in some instances this has proven impossible. The author and publisher will be glad to receive information leading to more complete acknowledgments in subsequent printings of the book and in the meantime extend their apologies for any omissions.

To AKW
The heart of it all.

# Contents

# Acknowledgments

*The Human Journalist: Reporters, Perspectives, and Emotions* is a compilation of insight and material from a wide variety of sources, some firsthand but many coming from the minds and pens of many gifted journalists and creative writers. As the book discusses, there are many different orientations to the journalistic profession and many different structures in which the stories are told. Equally there are many different viewpoints regarding journalists and the emotions they encounter—and experience themselves—during the course of their efforts to research and portray reality to their readers and viewers.

For their insight into these many perspectives, the author would like to thank the following people and sources. First and foremost is Col. Ann Norwood, M.D., a gifted psychiatrist who has worked with trauma victims and who compiled and presented the material presented as the afterword: Journalists and Traumatic Stress. For her chapter she interviewed a number of expert sources, including Dr. Frank Ochberg, a psychologist who has done a great amount of work with journalists and traumatic stress, Penny Owen, who covered the Oklahoma City bombing, and Mary Walsh, a senior news producer with CBS Television News.

Several times during the course of the chapters I will make reference to some extremely talented writers and writing coaches who represent the best in American journalism today. Among them are Rick Bragg, writer for the *New York Times;* Walt Harrington, former *Washington Post Magazine* writer and now professor of journalism at the University of Illinois; author Tom Wolfe; author and former *Sports Illustrated* reporter George Plimpton; the *Baltimore Sun's* Jon Franklin; writing coach Donald Fry;

Chip Scanlan, director of writing programs for the Poynter Institute of Media Studies; and at least one other important writer: Sebastian Junger. Of the journalistic works that have made the greatest positive impression on me over the past two decades, Junger's nonfiction book, *The Perfect Storm*, has made the greatest. Not only does Junger's reporting and writing style represent some of the best work in American journalism, especially given the limitations he operated under (all six victims of the tragedy were killed and could not relate their own account), page after page of his writing is a showcase of writing techniques that every writer should read. As I mention in the book, I have even used *The Perfect Storm* as a textbook in some of the writing courses I teach at the University of Memphis.

Certainly kudos also go to the editors and writers of *American Journalism Review* and *Columbia Journalism Review* for discussing journalistic issues such as the trauma occasioned by a journalist's witnessing tragedy in the making. The year 2001, with the fateful September 11 tragedy occurring in its midst, gave a living arena and reason for journalists to discuss that emotional issue.

I would also like to thank my graduate assistant, Simone Barden, for her help in researching this work.

Finally, I'd like to thank my wife, Anne, who brought insight to bear during my writing that is uncommonly sound regarding journalism, yet not all that atypical of thoughtful non-journalists who we in the newsrooms often underrate.

# Introduction: The Journalist's World

How important is the journalist to his or her society? If you believe research studies and you see television drama acted out in real life, for better or for worse, you come to feel the journalist is extremely important. President Thomas Jefferson took special note of the importance of the journalist's work in the burgeoning American society of the nineteenth century. He wrote that, were it left to him to choose a free government without a free press or a free press without a free government, he would not hesitate to choose the latter. His reasoning? No government is going to stay free for long without press freedom.

Do journalists know they hold individual reputations in their hands? Indeed they do. Do they know they could be dragged into libel court as a result of their honest efforts to enlighten society and expose the wrongs that need righting? Yes.

And do journalists understand that they can victimize a second time the people who have already experienced tragedy once? Did Lowell Bergman, formerly a producer with CBS's *60 Minutes*, know that in getting Dr. Jeffrey Wigand, a former senior scientist for Brown and Williamson Tobacco Company, to blow the whistle on the company, that he exposed him to legal jeopardy? Yes, Bergman knew that.

And do journalists understand that they are often asked to sign conflict-of-interest policies that may deter them from engaging in civic activity as innocent as voting or as publicly supporting a cause or movement? Yes, they do.

Do journalists realize the risk in simply forming strong friendships with nonjournalists: people they may be called upon to write about or use as sources one day? Do they understand some friendships may make them vulnerable to attempts at self-serving manipulation by those friends? Yes, they do.

Does a reporter understand that he or she is somehow expected to avoid feelings that any normal person might feel when witnessing tragedy or horror or in interviewing those who have experienced it? Does he know he could be criticized for allowing emotions to creep into his stories and that he may be labeled "sensationalistic" if he does? Yes, he knows it.

And do the reporter and editor know that they may be called upon to serve two different masters, such as the media corporation's stockholders and the consumers of the news, each of which may have radically different needs and requirements of the journalist? Yes, the journalist knows that as well.

Is the journalist aware that some of the best in the profession see journalism not as a job but as a mission in life; a mission that often keeps them away from their families for too long? And does she know that nonjournalists cannot often understand the intensity and love of chasing a story that a journalist experiences, thereby making it hard for the two to discuss their marital problems? Sadly, the journalist knows that as well.

And finally, does a journalist know that in trying to protect an innocent source in a story by keeping the name confidential, that he or she may be hauled into court and be cited for contempt, spending days or weeks in jail or facing a large fine for secreting the name of the source in a criminal trial? History has shown that journalists also know this.

These are just a few of the pressures journalists face in their world and a few of the reasons why their job is so hard, if not impossible at times. Were journalists the completely neutral, emotionless, robotic entities that some might like to be or that the job seems to demand they be, then these pressures wouldn't be so bad. But the reality is journalists are not robots; they are humans. Some are very, very human. They all love at one time or another; most know how to cry and some do it when they can get away with it. Many feel emotional pain when they witness tragedy or talk to others who have witnessed it, or, worse yet, lost loved ones in it. Some journalists get angry about what they see and hear; others get downright mad. Some wonder about why bad things seem to often happen to good people, like a little girl who is struck by a falling beam and killed as she sits in a church service next to her mommy on Sunday morning. Some journalists get frustrated at being lied to one too many times. Others want desperately to take sides on issues and champion what they believe in or cry out against perceived injustices.

They are basic, human emotions and journalists fall prey to them as much as anyone else in the world. Yet tradition says journalists must remain detached from all this and somehow be the neutral conduit—the medium—that connects the tragedies to the readers and viewers. Tradition says emotions can distort and color stories so they are no longer factual and objective. Tradition says journalists can, in fact, be objective. That they have the trained eyes and psyches that allow objects, events, people, and issues to somehow define themselves as the word "objectivity" says they do. The human journalist is asked to subdue his or her own perception of an object even while he or she describes that object. Just how is that supposed to be possible? Doesn't a person describe on the very basis of perception in the first place? And, being human, aren't perceptions human and therefore subject to an individual human's mental map?

*The Human Journalist: Reporters, Perspectives, and Emotions* is a study of these issues and more. It takes as a given that journalists are, in fact, human and that they do, in fact, experience emotions like everyone else. But it also realizes the special role journalists fill in society and the impact it might have on viewers if a trusted network news anchor panics on air or breaks into tears over the event or threat he or she is describing. It understands that, if a reporter leaves neutral reportage (if there is such a thing) and advocates an American withdrawal from a war, then personal value judgments are crowding out issues that can be seen from at least two opposing sides. Found on the editorial page, there is no problem with such a stance or approach. Finding it in the news columns is another matter altogether.

What should journalists do with the emotions they feel when doing their job in reporting the news? And what perspective, orientation, or approach should they take into that job in the first place? Should they remain detached from the action or get close to it and the people involved in it? Where is the trade-off between the safety that distance might provide versus the insight that involvement can offer? And what about the personal trauma visited upon reporters, photographers, and editors when they witness tragedy or fall victim to it themselves? Should they just bury it for fear they will somehow be seen by their peers as being less than effective—or less than neutral or accurate by their readers?

Being a journalist has never been easy. Journalists live in the same world as everyone else. Yet they inhabit a different professional world with requirements and options that can bind them or grate on them personally. That can lead to varying degrees of honesty, ethics, and accuracy in their finished stories. Journalists know their work impacts others—sometimes seriously. People have been known to commit suicide over fear of how they might be depicted in the press or over fear of being exposed. And journalists know that, while they present a representation of reality—a kind of shadow world—in their stories, the public and the authorities will react to that picture in the real world. It would be nice if the response were appropriate to the event itself. It would be nice if a country did not go to war, for example, over a misleading or false image. Historically, it would have been good if *The New York Journal's* insistence that Spain sank the Battleship *Maine* was verified before Teddy Roosevelt took his troops into battle in Cuba.

Reporters act on the basis of varying perspectives or approaches to their
craft that produce varying emotions inside them and in the readers and
viewers of their stories. Understanding this reality better is the goal of this
book.

*—Jim Willis*

# Chapter 1

# The Evolution of Journalism

At its best, journalism is an evolving craft and profession. It is not stationary but dynamic; not stagnant but always seeking to improve and grow. The best journalists learn from the successes and mistakes of the past, continue to assess how the society around them moves from one phase to the next, and seek out new and magnetic ways of reaching the readers who populate that society. Such is the history of American journalism. It is not only interesting but also instructive to see how reporting and writing have moved from one era to the next, sometimes improving...sometimes not.

As a writer and writing coach I have discovered the necessity of change when it comes not only to the presentation of material but also to the orientation that a journalist takes into the story in the first place. Chapter 2 will discuss some of these reporting orientations, and it is important to note there is no one uniform, monolithic way of reporting or writing the news. At any given point in contemporary journalism, there are several such perspectives at work. And in any given historical era there are also changes discernible in both the orientation to reporting as well as the presentation of the material collected.

That much is evident by looking through an anthology of stories such as Snyder and Morris's *Treasury of Great Reporting*.[1] This classic anthology collects wonderfully told stories dating back to the beginnings of American journalism and scrolling forward through centuries of solid and creative reporting and writing. Starting with stories such as "Hell in an Uproar" from a 1699 issue of *The London Spy,* and moving through pieces reported by Charles Dickens, B.S. Osborn, Mark Twain, Stephen Crane, John Reed, H.L. Mencken, Damon Runyan, Ernest Hemingway, Leland Stowe, Quentin Reynolds, William L. Shirer, A.J. Liebling, Rebecca West,

Ernie Pyle, and Marguerite Higgins, the editors do a fine job of showing how reporting and writing styles have changed over the centuries. Changed but, in some ways, staying the same.

In their introduction, the editors note:

The first and most obvious difference between reporting and other types of chronicling is the difference of *pace.* The reporter must have the ability to produce a rapid-fire story under conditions hardly ideal for creative writing. And to keep doing so...The change from horse-and-buggy and courier dispatch to jet planes and video has merely stepped up the reportorial pace.[2]

Indeed, as H. G. Wells once said, great reporting is the product of "an interrogative state of mind."[3] Reporters through the years, no matter what the prevailing writing style of the era, have continued to question, to probe, to look beyond the surface, to put a human face on even the most complex stories. At least that part of the reporting orientation does stay the same. What changes is how one might do the probing, what they might choose to probe in the first place, and how they might present those results for the reader or viewer.

Take, for example, the following two leads:

PORK CHOP HILL, KOREA, JAN. 3, 1953—Our Town atop Pork Chop Hill is in a world of its own.

Its contacts with the outside world are few—but imperative. Its immediate concern is the enemy on the next ridge. That's "His Town." To His Town, Our Town gives grudging respect. But, if possible, His Town is going to be wiped out.

Our Town's business is war. It produces nothing but death.[4]

NEW YORK CITY, JUNE 22, 1938—Listen to this, buddy, for it comes from a guy whose palms are still wet, whose throat is still dry, and whose jaw is still agape from the utter shock of watching Joe Louis knock out Max Schmeling.

It was a shocking thing, that knockout—short, sharp, merciless, complete. Louis was like this:

He was a big lean copper spring, tightened and retightened through weeks of training until he was one pregnant package of coiled venom.

Schmeling hit that spring .He hit it with a whistling right-hand punch in the first minute of the fight—and the spring, tormented with tension, suddenly burst with one brazen spang of activity.

Hard brown arms, propelling two unerring fists, blurred beneath the hot white candelabra of the ring lights. And Schmeling was in the path of them, a man caught and mangled in the whirring claws of a mad and feverish machine.[5]

While the Jim Lucas piece delivers the Korean action and the mood in concise, economic style, Bob Considine pumps plenty of adjectives and similes into his boxing story but still makes it sing. While Lucas conveys his story in a stark, realistic way, Considine delivers it with the breathless quality of a fan spewing out his beer at the corner bar after the fight. Clearly, there is no one best way to tell a story; no one best writing technique. In these two examples, if adjectives are poisonous, then one man's poison is definitely another man's meat.

So how has American journalism evolved over the years? Have the characteristics of the modern-day story always been thus? History says no.

## THE DIFFERENT LOOKS OF JOURNALISM

### Journalism as Opinion

The early newspapers in America published news and opinion interchangeably in their news hole. Both during the Colonial period and in the era of partisan journalism, which characterized American papers after the Revolutionary War, newspaper publishers often did little to separate the news and opinion function. Indeed, it is very doubtful that the American revolutionary cause could have succeeded without the partisan news support of these early newspapers. Early writers like Samuel Adams, who became known as the "assassin of reputations," often exaggerated facts about incidents involving British troops in the colonies. This reporting perspective, practiced widely by colonial editors and writers, was designed to polarize the occupying British forces and the colonials. It was designed to paint the British as all bad, and the colonials as all good.

The *Pennsylvania Journal and Weekly Advertiser* went so far as to frame its entire front page in a tombstone headed by a skull and crossbones on October 31, 1765, following the passage of the Stamp Act. That act, passed by the English government, provided that all legal documents, official papers, books, and newspapers should be printed on stamped paper that carried a special tax.

Boston became the hotbed of sedition, and the fire was fueled by partisan reporting in the *Boston Gazette,* printed by Benjamin Edes and John Gill. Edes was a member of the radical Sons of Liberty group, which John Adams referred to as the "Loyal Nine." During the summer of 1765 they printed the most bitter attacks on the Stamp Act that appeared in any colonial paper, and after the repeal they relented but little in their Patriot propaganda. The *Gazette* became the spokesman of the radicals.[6]

Another Boston paper that matched the *Gazette* stride for stride in propaganda was the *Massachusetts Spy,* founded by Isaiah Thomas. About Thomas, journalistic historian Frank Luther Mott wrote:

The original intention of the *Spy* was to be nonpartisan, and it carried a motto "Open to all Parties, but Influenced by None." Thomas was not slow, however, to discover that in these violent times neutrality was impossible...Political essays anonymously contributed, were abundant, and advocacy of independence was outspoken. The successive memorial observances of the anniversaries of the

Boston "massacre" were featured. In short, the Spy became the most incendiary publication in the colonies.[7]

Both the *Gazette* and the *Spy* were driven out of Boston by the threatening British but continued to publish in absentia.

On the other side of the Revolutionary period were editors like Hugh Gaine and James Rivington, the most hated of all the Tory editors. Gaine published the *New York Gazette and Weekly Mercury*, while Rivington published the *New-York Gazetteer*. Both were thoroughly partisan newspapers supporting the Tory cause.

Following the Revolutionary War, newspaper publishing flourished in the new states and about 450 new papers were begun in the 1780s and 1790s. Many of them were short-lived, while others lasted for a long time. Still, as Mott notes, the most obvious feature of journalism in this post-war period was its ardent partisan, political propaganda.[8] It was not surprising that political leaders should use newspapers to help them fight the battles that arose during the war between Federalists and Republicans.

Indeed one of the main reasons so many newspapers were born in this era was because political leaders funded them to voice their opinions and influence voters to support their causes. Journalism historians look at this era as the time of the Partisan Press; some refer to it as the Dark Age of American Journalism.

### Journalism as Sensationalism

The idea of sensationalism is not new. It was not invented by the *National Enquirer*, nor by the Fox Television network, nor any other twentieth century news organization. To some degree, sensationalism is as old as reporting but certainly as old as the mass-circulation daily newspaper. That predates even the 1890s Yellow Journalism era of Joseph Pulitzer and William Randolph Hearst and sends us looking back as far as the 1830s when newspaper publishers started realizing the value of news as entertainment to rope in readers. And a lot of them at that. As long as newspapers had been supported by political groups and audiences remained small, there wasn't much need to entice a large group of readers. But when Benjamin Day published his *New York Sun* in 1833 for a penny a copy and took in advertising for added revenue, the gate was opened for news as entertainment. Although Day's *Sun* was not that flashy, other entrants into the Penny Press era were. Those were newspapers like James Gordon Bennett's *New York Herald*, begun on May 6, 1835. "Shakespeare is the great genius of the drama," wrote Bennett in 1837, "Scott of the novel, Milton and Byron of the poem, and I mean to be the genius of the newspaper press."[9]

One of the hallmarks of sensationalism is a story that hypes the material beyond the facts and preys on the emotion of the reader or viewer. This was what Bennett's *Herald* did, for example, in building up the Robinson-Jewett murder trial to a level surpassing coverage of any other crime story to date. Bennett made it the first American murder story involving persons of no social standing to reach great newspaper proportions.[10] Helen Jewett, a prostitute, was found murdered in her room, and a young clerk named Robinson was tried for the crime. Bennett himself did some detective work on the case, became convinced of the prisoner's innocence, and devoted a lot of space to the coverage. Other papers followed the *Herald*'s lead, and the first real media circus was born. In the end, Robinson was acquitted, and the *Herald*'s circulation doubled during the trial.

In writing about Bennett and his sensationalism, journalism historian Frank Luther Mott wrote:

Bennett believed in advertising himself—"selling" his own personality to the public. He compared himself with Napoleon, with Moses. As a flamboyant self-advertiser, Bennett anticipated Barnum.[11]

But most historians feel sensationalism reached its zenith during the 1890s under Pulitzer and Hearst and their *New York World* and *New York Journal*. This was the so-called era of Yellow Journalism, given its name from the chief character in Richard F. Outcault's color comic strip, "The Yellow Kid." The toothless, mischievous grin on the kid's face became an appropriate symbol of this age when any pretense of objectivity was trampled upon in the name of newspaper competition between Hearst and Pulitzer. The news holes in both newspapers were turned into receptacles for some of the most outlandish, sensationalized reporting in history. Typical of the headlines and the stories that were to follow them were:

"Real American Monsters and Dragons"—over a story of the discovery of fossil remains by an archaeological expedition.

"A Marvelous New Way of Giving Medicine: Wonderful Results from Merely Holding Tubes of Drugs Near Entranced Patients."

"Strange Things Women Do for Love."

"Startling Confession of a Wholesale Murderer who Begs to be Hanged."

Sensationalism has continued to be a style of journalism through the 1800s, 1900s, and into the twenty-first century. It is a controversial style of reporting and writing that goes beyond letting the story speak for itself. In some television news and pseudo-news shows, sensationalism is characterized by overwriting, slow-motion video, musical soundtracks, and recreated events using actors in the roles of the real people. It is a concept that describes the way a story is told more than the issue of taking liberty with the facts. Sensationally told stories may, in fact, stay close to the facts;

but the way these stories are told exaggerates some of these points and adds its own emotional mood to the story.

## Journalism as Fact

Just as there have always been elements of entertainment in news reporting, so has there always been an element of factuality to it. The degree to which those facts are honored has, however, varied from era to era as the preceding section shows. The American public began tiring in the 1890s of the blatant sensationalism and distortions of fact that came to characterize the newspapers of Joseph Pulitzer and William Randolph Hearst. The *New York Times* was emerging as a paper devoted to factual reporting, and it was this kind of no-nonsense journalism that many Americans found appealing after the comic-book nature of newspapers emulating the *New York Journal* and *New York World*.

Semanticist S. I. Hayakawa distinguishes three different types of writing as judgment, inference, and report writing. The last is the most neutral, albeit at times the most colorless, of the three. This is the style of reporting that Adolph Ochs had his *New York Times* practicing as the century drew to a close, and the style was also apparent in a growing number of daily newspapers around the country. Ochs himself declared the operating principles and goals of the *Times* when he wrote:

It will be my earnest aim that the *New York Times* give the news, all the news in concise and attractive form, in language that is parliamentary in good society, and give it as early, if not earlier, than it can be learned through any other reliable medium; to give the news impartially, without fear or favor, regardless of any party, sect or interest involved; to make the columns of the *New York Times* a form for the consideration of all questions of public importance and to that end to invite intelligent discussion from all shades of opinion.[12]

Neutrality and fairness, or at least the attempt at achieving both, were guiding principles of factual journalism. The inverted-pyramid format of storytelling was born during the tumultuous and unpredictable Civil War years as correspondents tried to get their stories filed over the wires before the opposing army cut them. It became the chief way in which factual journalism was conveyed to the public. Facts themselves, as opposed to yarns, became the basis of this brand of objectivity in American journalism. This would come to characterize serious, mainstream American newspaper journalism for a long time and, indeed, still is at the center of much American journalism today. There would be exceptions, throwback eras to Yellow Journalism such as the 1920s era of Jazz Journalism in Chicago and New York, but factual journalism was becoming the standard of serious newspaper journalism as this century began.

## Journalism as Propaganda

With the coming of troubles in Europe and with the growing debate of whether the United States should insert itself into a foreign war, the federal government discovered journalism could be a useful propaganda tool. Actually, this was not a new discovery at all, as Sam Adams, the Sons of Liberty, and the Committees on Correspondence had shown in American revolutionary days. Journalism had also been a driving force for getting America involved with the war with Spain after the U.S. Battleship Maine was sunk in Havana.

But America had seen nothing like the conscription of journalism that took place during the presidential administration of Woodrow Wilson. To counter the popular opposition to entering the war in Europe, President Wilson created the Committee on Public Information (CPI), headed by muckraking newspaper editor George Creel, to flood the country with war propaganda. Journalists even of the stature of Walter Lippmann required little arm-twisting to play the role Wilson asked of the American press. As Robert Karl Manoff notes, "the press not only supported the war...but did so on the terms established by the state."[13]

Reflecting on this mobilization effort, Lippmann called it the single most effective effort in history at creating one unified public opinion. He described the effort this way:

Probably this is the largest and the most intensive effort to carry quickly a fairly uniform set of ideas to all the people of a nation. The older proselytizing worked more slowly, perhaps more surely, but never so inclusively. Now if it required such extreme measures to reach everybody in time of crisis, how open are the more normal channels to men's minds? The Administration was trying, and while the war continued it very largely succeeded in creating something that might almost be called one public opinion all over America...Nothing like that exists in time of peace, and as a corollary there are whole sections, there are vast groups, ghettoes, enclaves and classes that hear only vaguely about much that is going on.[14]

## Journalism as Interpretation

Some historians feel the Great Depression caused the American news media to take a harder look at its role as interpreter of events and issues. Many Americans were shocked over the news of the stock market collapse in 1929, and many blamed journalists for not alerting them to the coming event. If true, it could be the media of the day was hamstrung by either a strict adherence to fact or a leaning toward the so-called Jazz Journalism of the era. This was a round of crime and scandal sensationalism akin to the Yellow Journalism of the 1890s. In any event, the idea of divining meaning or interpreting daily events for their future impact was not a mainstream journalistic thought.

Helping to alter the focus was a journalism textbook called, *Interpretive Reporting,* written by Curtis MacDougall and published first in 1938. MacDougall and a growing number of editors posited the idea that the reporter's job is not complete in simply describing the who, what, when, where, and how of a news event. More attention should be paid to the "why" question and to the significance of the event to related events and issues. In years to follow, other journalists like William Rivers would insist that news reporting is inseparable from interpretation. Often, Rivers said, reporters interpret in making what might seem to be simple, factual statements. For example, if a reporter describes someone as tall, he or she is using his own standard for tallness, and that standard changes depending on how short or tall the reporter is himself or herself.

Interpretation is different from editorializing because when a reporter interprets, he or she is only looking for connections and patterns; he or she is not making a statement of opinion or a value judgment. A reporter may say this pattern or that pattern exists, but she will not generally make a value judgment about that pattern.

### Journalism as Stenography

When are journalists like stenographers or court reporters? When they simply transcribe what they are told, attribute the statement to the source, then make little if any effort to verify the information. Such was the case in this country's history when Sen. Joseph McCarthy took advantage of the Communist scare in the early 1950s to further his career by alleging the State Department and the Army were full of Communist sympathizers. Every day brought new charges of Communist infiltration from the senator, whose number of infiltrators seemed to change almost daily. There were so many charges, in fact, that the press found it difficult to keep up with them, let alone check them out. McCarthy knew what he was doing. He had effectively enlisted the support of the news media in pressing his case, spurious and overblown as it was. It was as if this episode in history was a three-ring circus with Joe McCarthy as the ringmaster and many journalists his trained lions. Those journalists who participated were often just following a standard notion of objective reporting and writing at the time: that you simply take down what is said, attribute it back to the source, and your job is done. The idea of verification was a good one if there were time, but, if not, go with what you've got. It was fertile ground for a manipulative United States senator who knew how journalists defined news value.

To subscribe to this simplistic type of journalism is to have journalists cast themselves as little more than stenographers, taking down notes accurately but doing little to insure that what they are printing is the truth. Journalistic historians have looked back on this era of journalism and labeled it "straightjacket journalism" with the source tying the knot that held the jacket in place.

## Journalism as Investigation

Perhaps it was the lesson of straightjacket journalism or perhaps it was just journalism coming of age, but the 1960s and 1970s was the time for investigative journalism to shine and bring a needed dimension to the journalism of the 1950s. It wasn't as if journalists hadn't practiced investigative journalism before. But in the 1830s, 1890s, and 1920s, investigative reporting was often linked to manipulative efforts by newspaper publishers like James Gordon Bennett, William Randolph Hearst, and magazine publisher Frank McClure to sell more newspapers and magazines. The investigative journalism that was characterized by the Watergate episode and hard-hitting Vietnam reporting was separated from the bottom-line efforts of newspapers and sometimes in conflict with those efforts.

This was expensive journalism in more ways than one. Investigative reporters were taken out of the daily loop of producing stories and were allowed to spend long periods of time pursuing one story that might not surface for weeks or months. And when those stories were published, there was always the danger of libel as these reporters majored in uncovering corruption and illegalities. Further, because these stories were so in-depth, they often ran much longer than the normal news story, and readers are often turned off by long stories. Additionally, many of the issues these stories dealt with involved complex business and government stories on topics that weren't too exciting for a lot of readers. And there was always the risk these newspapers encountered in putting their credibility on the line.

So this kind of investigative reporting was carried out much more as a service, as part of a journalist's implied Constitutional mandate, than as a means of selling the newspaper product. And this journalism was built upon intrepid research, documentation, and verification. Investigative journalists focused on content more than storytelling; the stories may have been dry reading for some, but the information they delivered was sorely needed by society.

## Journalism as Literature

Out of the counterculture movement of the 1960s and 1970s came a desire on the part of many journalists to dress up the rather staid journalistic forms and structures associated with strict adherence to the inverted pyramid and rather sterile, arms-length reporting tactics. Leading this movement were writers like Tom Wolfe and Hunter S. Thompson, perhaps with an inspirational boost from wacky (some say approaching the level of genius) media guru Marshal McLuhan. It was McLuhan who coined the phrase, "the medium is the message," and later tweaked it to read enigmatically, "the medium is the massage."

This perspective on journalism believed that the way the message was written was just as important as what the message said, for it was often in the writing that the nuances of the message came through the strongest to the reader. If a journalist had to borrow writing techniques from other realms, such as fiction, so much the better if he or she came up with a better told story in the process.

This was the so-called New Journalism of the age, and it split reporter from reporter and editor from editor, much as the American Civil War had done to families over much larger issues. Editors who worshipped at the altar of the inverted pyramid grew irate over reporters' attempts to dress up their writing in a literary suit. Reporters tired of the old ways, chafed at sterilizing their copy into formulaic structures and insisted on experimenting with new forms.

If one were to take Tom Wolfe as the guiding light of this style of journalism, he or she would have the following principles to shine as a torch:

- Careful scene-by-scene construction; a kind of social autopsy of the minutest details in relevant scenes.
- A lot of dialogue. Some of the best quotes come when characters in your story are speaking to each other rather than to the reporter or narrator.
- A kind of imperialistic reporting that goes deep into the thinking, feelings, and motivations of the characters involved in the story.
- A lot of description and abundant use of anecdotes showing characters in action and using those actions and vignettes to illustrate larger points.
- A narrative form of writing, building from the minute to the climax, rather than vice versa as the inverted pyramid does.
- Use of reporter impressions; how the characters and scenes feel to the writer or narrator.

Critics of literary journalism asked, "Where is the baseline for this type of reporting? How do you verify that your impressions are correct?" Supporters of this brand of journalism simply noted the baseline is in the research itself and in the integrity of the researcher and writer. In other words, you have to select good reporters and then trust them to do their job.

### Journalism as Advocacy

Another part of the counterculture movement was advocacy journalism, a modern-day throwback to the crusading journalism of the nineteenth and early twentieth centuries. An advocacy journalist is one who goes beyond the line of objectivity to promote or champion a particular cause, or, conversely, to point out the flaws of a disliked cause. The birth of modern-day advocacy journalism can probably be traced to the alternative and underground press of the 1960s and 70s. Publications like *The Berkeley Barb* in California or *The Village Voice* in New York City felt the minority voices—often the voices for radical change—were being snuffed out by the conservative, mainstream press that, overall, promoted the status quo in society. So, with these radical causes absent a voice, the alternative press decided to give them one and speak for causes such as civil liberties and the environment. To advocacy journalists this is not a sellout to public relations; it is rather providing a needed alternative voice to the mainstream press, often too controlled by powerful corporate interests seeking to promote the status quo.

Perhaps in environmental journalism we still see this debate over advocacy journalism still being played out. In covering that beat, not every journalist agrees on how environmental reporters should orient themselves. Many believe the beat should be handled no differently from any other one a reporter approaches. They believe a strict objective stance is necessary, with the journalists taking care not to take sides in the issues covered. But others believe environmental reporters have an additional responsibility in reporting the story and should assume the role of advocates for cleaning up the environment, or at least maintaining it, and making sure the government notices the problems and takes steps to solve them. "Conservation" is a watchword among many environmental journalists.

The Society of Environmental Journalists itself seems split over the debate. Numbering some 1,000 journalists, many of this group remain dedicated to a traditional objective stance, while others have crossed over into advocacy territory. One writer once said he feels the SEJ is more concerned about marketing the environment and hyping environmental problems beyond the actual risks associated with them.[15] The SEJ sees huge threats involved in such issues as nuclear waste disposal, hazardous spills and waste disposals, and the hole in the ozone layer. Like most avid reporters, they are deeply concerned about the problems they write about and feel closer to them than the general public. But to some journalists, this poses a problem as writer Alston Chase wrote:

By hyping environmental problems, society is often less than tolerant toward those who doubt the severity of these putative crises. Its meetings are largely love feasts. And this conformity tends to make the field both boring and irrelevant, negating the promotional efforts of the faithful. Like much environmental press coverage, SEJ's national meetings have become exercises in orthodoxy, where true believers reign and dissenters are denigrated.[16]

Indeed, at its 1995 national meeting, SEJ Conference Chair David Ropeik told the newsletter *Environmental Writer*, "We're trying to put the environment on the political agenda of the United States."[17]

Rebutting Chase's charges, SEJ President Emily Askari said the organization is committed to improving the quality, accuracy, and visibility of environmental journalism. Still, Dr. Michael Frome, former conservation editor of *Field and Stream*, columnist for the Los Angeles times and author of several books on the environment has urged environmental reporters to "write from the heart." He believes the motivation should be to show the intangible values of the human heart and spirit and how living in harmony with nature can only lead to living in harmony with each other.[18]

This debate over advocacy journalism is not, of course, limited to environmental reporting. It is an issue with many journalistic beats, and some feel the debate is fanned by the existence of so many specialized organizations of journalists, formed around the beats or ethnicities they cover. Thus there is the National Association of Science Writers, Society of American Business and Economic Writers, Investigative Reporters and Editors, the National Association of Black Journalists, National Association of Native American Journalists, National Association of Gay and Lesbian Writers, National Association of Hispanic Journalists, National Association of Asian-American Journalists, and the list goes on. By seeing yourself as separate and distinct from other journalists on other beats, critics charge, you set yourself up to align more closely with the causes of those you cover than to remain detached from them. Others simply believe this threat comes with the territory of specialization, and honest reporters will remain objective.

### Journalism as Entertainment

Is there anyone in America today who has not seen the blurring of the lines between news and entertainment? Whether we're talking newspapers, magazines, television, or books, entertainment is often the fuel that drives the money machine of even the most serious of news organizations. Reams have been written about how even CBS, ABC and NBC nightly newscasts have gone softer in subject matter. Reporter Leslie Stahl of *60 Minutes* once told Bill Moyers, "I like to wallpaper my stories with pretty pictures," and said this is more and more the requirement from network producers.[19]

But the entertainment issue goes far beyond how a reporter packages a story. After all, television is a visual medium, so obviously it pays strict attention to its wallpaper. Newspapers are doing the same with the influx of color and innovative design strategies where form often holds sway over function in the interest of enticing the reader to the stories inside. The rub about entertainment in the news industry is what stories and what people get covered in the first place, and how that coverage is handled. How many times have respected reporters like dismissed *Boston Globe* columnist Mike Barnicle and respected news programs like NBC's *Date-*

*line* crossed the line in either making up sources or quotes or in going all out to rig an event to climax as they want it to?

Book after book has chronicled the blurring of the news and entertainment lines and chided news organizations for giving in. Neil Postman's *Amusing Ourselves to Death* was one classic, but even that was preceded by an amazingly prophetic 1960s book, *The Image: A Guide to Pseudo-Journalism in America*, by Daniel Boorstin. In his book, Boorstin explained that many news media, most notably television, strive to satisfy the viewer's craving to see something more bizarre and dramatic than they saw yesterday. America is yearning for the image, he said, and the media are striving to give it to them.[20] The problem is they are finding it in pseudo-events, or those events that are designed to be dramatic and entertaining. The problem is they are devoid of substance, and the media delivers the shadows instead. The focus on celebrity news is only one example of this pseudo-journalism. It can be found anytime journalists chase stories without substance in order to deliver entertainment to the audience.

## Journalism as Storytelling

Go to any journalistic writer's conference these days and you will hear Pulitzer Prize–winning journalists talking about "storytelling." You will hear little to nothing about the inverted pyramid or other traditional news story formats. You will hear little to nothing about distancing yourself as a writer from the story or the sources. In fact, those sources are often referred to as story characters, much the same as novel characters would be. But wait a second...aren't we back to talking about the 1960s brand of New Journalism? The answer is no, despite the desire to embrace literary techniques used in other writing genres. The main difference between this new emphasis on storytelling and the 1960s New Journalism of Tom Wolfe is its concrete focus on facts and the one indelible rule of never inventing or changing facts.

Perhaps the best example of this kind of storytelling, in book form anyway, is Sebastian Junger's *The Perfect Storm*. In his commentary on his book, Junger said it was his desire to tell a story in a very engaging and entertaining way while still honoring one cardinal rule: never invent any facts, and never invent any dialogue or direct quotes. Within these restrictions, Junger works wonders in crafting a magnetic read about a fishing crew lost at sea in the storm of the century.

Some leading journalists have referred to this kind of journalistic storytelling as "intimate journalism." Writer Walt Harrington uses that term and explains it as follows:

The simple goal of intimate journalism should be to describe and evoke how people live and what they value. That short phrase encompasses the full range of our lives—work, children, faith, anything that we do or that we believe important, everything ordinary and everything extraordinary in our lives. I'm talking about a kind of story that rises and falls on narrative structure, the reporting of physical detail, the reporting of human emotion, on evocative tone and the pulling of thematic threads through the course of the story. It's a journalism rooted in descriptive journalism.[21]

Harrington describes the basic techniques of intimate journalism as follows:

- Thinking, reporting and writing in scenes.
- Capturing a narrator's voice and/or writing the story from the point of view of one or several subjects...trying to evoke their felt lives.
- Gathering telling details from our subjects' lives, details that evoke the tone of that life...trying to report through all five of our senses.
- Gathering real-life dialogue. It creates the sense of life happening before readers' eyes.
- Gathering interior monologue—what subjects are thinking, feeling, imagining, dreaming, worrying about or wondering to themselves...focusing not only on the facts but on the meaning that the facts have for our subjects.
- Reporting to establish a time line that will allow us to write a narrative article that at its beginning posits a problem, dilemma or tension that will be resolved or relieved by the end of the story, with a resultant change in our main subject or subjects. This gives the story a beginning, a middle, and an end.
- Immersing ourselves temporarily in the lives of our subjects so they become relaxed in our presence and so we can see real events unfold, develop and be resolved.
- Gathering physical details of places and people.
- Always being aware that no matter how artful our stories may be, how specific they are to the lives our subjects, they are primarily meant to enlighten, caution, criticize or inspire, always resonate, in the lives of readers. The eternal verities of love, hate, fear, ambition, dedication, compassion are still our bread and butter.
- Finally, the glue for all of this is the reader's belief that, as Tom Wolfe once said, All of this is true! It's all true—the color of hair and eyes, the raising of an eyebrow or a pause in mid-sentence, the details of a private reverie.

## SUMMARY

All of this then takes us back to our opening thoughts in this chapter: that American journalism is not a static or one-dimensional art form. It continues to go through changes, adapts and evolves to different eras and conditions within those eras. It learns from itself; from its mistakes and miscues, and it tries to push ahead and improve on those mistakes. Each adaptation has something to offer the next, either in positive or negative lessons.

The evolution of journalism as opinion, sensationalism, fact, interpretation, stenography, investigation, literature, advocacy, entertainment, and storytelling makes this craft a fascinating career for writers. It is important to note that no one of these eras has a corner on journalism. Instead, all of these concepts compete at the same time in any single era for the attention of readers and viewers. Today, for example, we see numerous examples simultaneously of journalism as entertainment, journalism as investigation, journalism as sensationalism, journalism as interpretation, and journalism as storytelling.

The next chapter offers a closer look at these and other perspectives that journalists take into their craft and profession. As you will see, there is room in American journalism for a variety of approaches and perspectives to the business of informing the public about people, events, and issues important and interesting to their daily lives.

## NOTES

1. Louis Snyder and Richard Morris, *The Treasury of Great Reporting* (New York: McGraw-Hill, 1969), 230.

2. Ibid.

3. Ibid.

4. Jim Lucas, Scripps-Howard, 3 January 1953.

5. Bob Considine, International News Service, 22 June 1938.

6. Frank Luther Mott, *The History of American Journalism* (Bloomington: Indiana University Press, 1972), 127.

7. Ibid, 77–78.

8. Ibid, 113.

9. Ibid, 229.

10. Ibid, 233.

11. Ibid, 235.

12. William David Sloan, James G. Stovall, and James D. Startt, *The Media in America: A History,* (Worthington, Ohio: Publishing Horizons, Inc., 1989), 233.

13. Robert Karl Manoff, comments made at the seminar, "War, Peace, and the News Media," sponsored by the Gannett Foundation and New York University, New York City, 19 March 1983.

14. Walter Lippmann, *Public Opinion* (New York: Macmillan, 1922), 22.

15. Allston Chase, "Do Environmental Journalists Really Exist?" *Detroit News,* 31 August 1995, 8.

16. Ibid.

17. Ibid.

18. Emily Askari, "Rebuttal: Chase Criticism of Journalists Unfounded," *Detroit News,* 10 October 1995, 9.

19. Leslie Stahl, "Illusions of News," comments to Bill Moyers, *The Public Mind*, PBS, 1989.

20. Daniel Boorstin, *The Image: A Guide to Pseudo-Journalism in America* (New York: Atheneum, 1985), 2.

21. Walt Harrington, *Intimate Journalism: The Art and Craft of Reporting Everyday Life* (Thousand Oaks, Calif: Sage, 1997), xix.

# Chapter 2

# Seeking the Best Seat in the House

You have special advance tickets to the best road show in town and are excited about the opportunity to experience it and later review it. Perhaps it is *Phantom, Rent,* or *Les Miserables.* What makes your tickets special is that they allow you to select your seats yourself. You can view the action—or even be a part of it—from any vantage point possible. Perhaps you choose the loge boxes; perhaps the front row. Or perhaps you prefer a more detached, sweeping view of the action by heading to the mezzanine. Or maybe you're attending a play that allows seating on the stage itself. You become an extra as a patron in the bistro setting of the play.

Probably the seat you select will be the one that allows you the vantage point you are seeking because you believe that perspective or orientation will give you the most realistic and accurate view of the action and the characters involved in it. It will be one that enhances the moment, provides the right mood, and sets your creative juices free to experience the play as it should be.

In short, you are seeking the best seat in the house. And you realize that your best seat may not be the same one selected by another reviewer. This is the seat that is best for you. It is best for your own unique understanding of your role as a drama critic and for what you want your readers to glean from your review.

Shakespeare reminded us that all the world is a stage and all the people are merely actors who make their entrances, perform their roles, then exit. It does not seem far-fetched, therefore, to expand this analogy of drama critic to the reporter at large who covers more real and influential events, issues, and people in the world. As does the drama critic, the everyday reporter is always seeking the best seat in the house to report as accurately as possible.

As a professor of journalism I have often found myself dealing with the following attitude among journalism majors: "I'm going into public relations, because I just don't have the attitude needed to become a reporter." When I press these students on what kind of attitude that is, they usually reply with sometime like, "Oh, you know, the hard-headed, emotionless person who will do anything to get a story—usually a sensational one— no matter who gets hurt." The actual responses vary, but the content remains about the same. The prevailing thought is there is only one orientation toward reporting, only one perspective, and that is of a stereotypical sort of investigative or tabloid journalist. When I suggest to them there are other orientations they could take into journalism, they often grow curious and want to know more.

Many years ago, while a graduate student at the University of Missouri, I was pondering reporting orientations myself. In reflecting on my years in the news business, it seemed I had come across several that differed from the stereotypical ones. I decided to do a little research on the topic and, before long, I had convinced myself there are many different orientations or perspectives to this craft. I also convinced myself that journalism is much better because of it.

After sorting out and identifying the various perspectives, I assigned names to each to make it easier to visualize them and their distinctions. Over the years I have changed and added to this list, which now encompasses the following perspectives, a couple named for individuals who might typify these approaches: the *Joe Friday, George Plimpton, Scientific, Impressionistic, Investigative, Friendly Eye, Pseudo, Village, Economic, Virtual, Advocacy, Larger Truth, and Storyteller* orientations. The rest of this chapter will discuss each of these perspectives and show how each contributes to the rich, multi-layered texture of American journalism.

## THE ORIENTATIONS

From the most traditional to the variations and extremes of that approach, the various reporting orientations or perspectives are as follows, starting with the no-nonsense Joe Friday perspective.

### The Joe Friday Approach

The naming of this first orientation was growing rather dated when Dan Ackroyd reminded Americans in the 1990s about the famed, stoic hero of the old *Dragnet* television series; then the series itself was reborn in 2002. Joe Friday was the traditionalist's traditionalist. He was the quintessential no-nonsense, single-minded, uniformly focused cop on the L.A.

beat. He seemed to live for one thing and one thing only: to catch the crook. Nothing got in his way of doing this, as long as his operating boundaries were standard operating police procedures of the day. He would not venture outside those limits, but he was tireless within them.

If there is one line, more than any other, that typified Joe Friday as he interviewed witnesses and suspects it was, "Just the facts, Ma'am." He had no time for the pointless casual conversation, unless it were a short one with his partner Frank Gannon who tried to add a little levity to Friday's emotionless statue. And if there were extenuating circumstances that caused his prey to become involved in a crime, it wasn't Friday's job to hear about it. That was for someone else down the line, after the bust was made.

You could fast-forward this character to the one played by Tommie Lee Jones in the movie *The Fugitive* in the mid-1990s. Jones's character, Deputy Sam Gerrard, was only slightly more multi-dimensional than Jack Webb's Joe Friday had been. The intensity was the same, the single focus was the same, and the no-nonsense approach was the same.

Transferring this approach over to the world of journalism, you come up with the classic hard news reporter of the twentieth century. The one who believes objectivity is truly possible and does his or her best to prove it in the way he or she operates. The one who worships at the altar of the inverted pyramid in writing his or her story and who embraces the most neutral verbiage possible. For example, the attributive verb "said" is the verb of choice over the more subjective ones like "asserted," "laughed," "demanded," or "argued." Using verbs such as these allows reporters too much latitude to opine, the Joe Fridays of the reporting world say. Stick instead to neutral ground, no matter how bland or nonspecific the verb "said" might be.

The Joe Friday reporter believes deeply in separating himself or herself from the story being covered. Never would you find such a reporter showing emotional involvement in the story, and never would you find him or her sampling the action to sense what the actual characters are sensing and feeling. Never would you find the Joe Friday reporter telling a story from the first person, and seldom would you find him or her telling it from the second-person viewpoint. The third person, the "he," "she," or "it" perspective, is always the best because it is the most detached.

As far as reporter allegiance is concerned, the paramount loyalty for the Joe Friday reporter is the accurate story. It is important to note, however, that we're using "accurate" and not "truthful" as the adjective here. To many Joe Friday types, going for the truth is going on a search that is best done by someone else. Remember the scene in *The Fugitive,* for example, when Gerrard is chasing Dr. Richard Kimball through the underground storm sewer? Kimball gets the momentary upper hand, and, aiming Gerrard's own gun at the deputy, announces, "I didn't kill my wife!" To which

Gerrard replies, "I don't care!" Gerrard's mission was something less than finding the truth of the situation; it was simply to catch the fugitive and let others decide his guilt or innocence. To be fair, this analogy breaks down a bit when it comes to reporters, because most do really care about the truth; they just don't always have time to plumb it and must go for a lesser goal of accuracy.

This is much the same with the Joe Friday reporter who sees the job as one of finding the facts of the situation and laying them out for the reader to decide. Roger Rosenblatt noted in a *Time* magazine essay, "Journalism and the Larger Truth," that finding the larger truth is beyond the pale of the everyday journalist. Rather, her job is to find the facts and to print or air them. The truth is in the purview of others such as writers of books, philosophers, clergy, or individuals in deep conversation with one another. Asking the journalist to find the truth of a situation or issue is asking too much, he concludes.[1]

Accuracy, on the other hand, is somewhat easier to latch onto and deliver. Here all you must do is find knowledgeable sources, interview them, and quote them accurately. It certainly helps if you can spot discrepancies in their statements and question them about these inconsistencies, but that's about as far as it goes. Interpreting their remarks in light of other factors and then piecing all that information into a big-picture story that goes for the larger truth . . . well, that's not the job of the daily reporter.

The problem, of course, is that accuracy does not always equal truth. A person may be quoted accurately, but that person may be mistaken in what he is saying. Or he may just flat-out be lying.

Maintaining arms-length detachment from a story is also important to the Joe Friday reporter. Becoming a part of the action, or getting too close to the sources, or pumping emotion into the story are inconsistent with this reporter's goal of objectivity. And they threaten that goal, by making the reporter feel for one side or the other in a conflict. Better to stay emotionally distanced.

The Joe Friday Approach to reporting is an important one. It has helped make journalists the independent voice they often are and has helped steel them against attempts to pressure or influence them by persons or groups with special interests. But there are also problems with this iron-clad approach, not the least of which is the belief that a reporter can truly remain objective, especially in a story involving a lot of swirling emotions. The trappings of objectivity (inverted-pyramid structure, third-person viewpoint, neutral verbiage, and so forth) may be there, but the real attitude of objectivity is something harder—if not impossible—to implement. Also problematic is the belief that a story reads truer, or at least most accurately, if it is devoid of emotional expression. Or, for that matter, if the reporter distances himself or herself emotionally from it. Suppose, for example, that the story is *about* emotions? Then does refusing to feel what others may be feeling really add to the accuracy of the story? Or does it subtract from it?

In certain breaking-news situations, this approach to reporting is great. In other situations, where more sensitivity and empathy are needed in order to transport readers or viewers to the scene, this approach is handicapped. By refusing to bring all of a reporter's senses (both physiological and emotional) into a story, it is highly possible that the real story will wind up being distorted, especially in presenting an accurate mood of the event or issue, or people involved.

To deal with this problem and to gain more insight into what people are really going through in crucible situations, other perspectives have been developed. One of them I call the George Plimpton Approach to reporting.

## The George Plimpton Approach

When *Sports Illustrated* writer George Plimpton decided to don the uniform of a Detroit Lion's quarterback to see how difficult it was for a rookie to make the team, he was engaging in participative journalism. He was not the first, nor the last to do it. The famed Nellie Bly (Elizabeth Cochrane) had done the same when she went inside an insane asylum, disguised as a patient, to see what life was like for patients there. And Dan Rather did it when he went into Afghanistan disguised as a rebel to see what life was like for the fighters there.

But Plimpton's style of journalism is characterized by this participative approach to journalism. It is his belief that, if you really want to "hear the roar of the greasepaint and the smell of the crowd," then you have to don that greasepaint and get in front of that crowd. What you give up, in terms of arms-length objectivity, you more than gain in terms of understanding and empathy. Both these, in turn, help to portray a more truthful account of what life is like for those in the center of the storm.

Plimpton's participative journalism is close in style to the anthropologist's approach of studying the lives of a culture up close and personal, often living with them for months or more to get a definitive portrait or case study. A few journalists bridge the gap between anthropology and journalism. One such self-defined "storytelling anthropologist" is Richard Critchfield who wrote often of how he covered news in foreign countries and of how that coverage differs from traditional journalism. A former reporter for the *Economist* and the *Washington Star,* Critchfield broke out of tradition when he embarked on his orientation as a storytelling anthropologist years ago. His goal was to cover what was really happening in Third-World countries. He felt the best way to do that was to get away from the nation's capitals and move out where the people live and work. He felt he had to become involved with them, their work, and their daily lives.

Critchfield believes most of the world's struggles bubble up from the hard times Third-World nations have in adapting to Western technology, ideas, and values. A later perspective to be outlined, the Village Approach, will delve in more detail into Critchfield's approach.

The clash of reporting styles—the traditional arms-length approach versus the participative approach—was depicted in the 1983 film *The Year of Living Dangerously*. The film takes place in Jakarta in the 1960s when fictional Australian broadcaster Guy Hamilton learns the secret of truthful and effective reporting from Eurasian photojournalist Billy Kwan. That secret, Kwan shows him, is found in avoiding the official story and instead going to the people impacted by those policies. In one telling scene where Kwan performs an impromptu puppet show for Hamilton one evening, Kwan tells the reporter that to understand the puppets, he must first understand the shadows on the wall that the puppets cast.

In another scene from that same film, Hamilton and Kwan are strolling one evening through the squalor of Jakarta. Kwan suggests that five American dollars would be a fortune to these people to which Hamilton replies, "Journalists just can't afford to get involved." Kwan points out that this is the traditional Western journalist's view but reminds Hamilton that Leo Tolstoy had a different tack, asking, "What then must we do?" Kwan concluded he believes journalists—like everyone else—must "add their light to the sum of light" and help where they can.

The participative approach—whether of the kind practiced by George Plimpton, Leo Tolstoy, or the fictional Kwan—is not for every journalist. It threatens the detachment that many feel is imperative. But it offers an interesting, alternative orientation for those who do follow it.

### The Scientific Approach

For some journalists, not only is the participative approach too radical a stance to take as a journalist, but even the traditional approach doesn't quite do the job. These journalists are influenced strongly by methods of behavioral scientists who try to isolate variables and produce conclusions with statistical teeth to them. In this approach, the journalist comes closest to using the methodology employed by the scientist. Championed by such journalistic scholars as Philip Meyer in his book *The New Precision Journalism*, this approach insists that reporters must have better documentation if their stories are going to be called accurate. The best documentation, they say, is found in quantitative research techniques such as those used by social and behavioral scientists. They include the random sample survey, content analysis, and controlled field experiments. By understanding and adapting these methods to reporting, the journalist is better able to explain and predict trends or events happening in society.

Meyer notes the following about one of the media's now-common research practices, polling:

To defend against being manipulated, the media need more self-confidence, and the best route to self-confidence is through knowledge. Media polls proliferated in the 1980s precisely because the editors no longer trusted the polls that politicians tried to give them and armed themselves with their own data-collection operations out of self-defense. Thus polling became not so much a way to make news as an enhanced tool of the newsgathering process itself.[2]

Maxwell McCombs has referred to this orientation as "social indicator reporting."[3] In following its method, an everyday beat reporter can be on observance for a multitude of social indicators that are kept by myriad government agencies in the form of monthly, quarterly, or annual reports or statistics. Marriage, divorce, bankruptcy, death, crime, and building-permit statistics are examples of these records accessible to all reporters. Tracked over time and compared with other similar time periods, these social indicators can offer a more comprehensive picture of what is happening in society. Applying some simple statistical analysis to these indicators can deepen that documentation as well as the predictive capacity of those trends discovered.

To critics, this approach is too sterile and devoid of the human element that must be so much a part of journalistic stories. To supporters, it is a reporting approach that offers solid documentation to those stories. This approach will be detailed in chapter 4.

## The Impressionistic Approach

If you were looking for a reporting orientation that is the polar opposite of the Scientific Approach, it would have to be the Impressionistic Approach. Like the Plimpton Approach, this perspective values how the story is told almost as much as what the story has to say. There is a strong literary tradition found here, as introduced in chapter 1, that often gets reduced to formulaic writing in the Friday Approach. Yet most of the reporters coming to this style of writing, popularized by journalist/novelist Tom Wolfe, do not go as far as Plimpton might in becoming a physical part of the action. Instead, they seek its realism through a combination of techniques including:

- Sparing no effort as a reporter in trying to invade the psyche of the person being interviewed. This has sometimes been dubbed imperialistic reporting by some because there is a sense of invading territory that doesn't belong to you.

- Recording the most minute mannerisms of the speaker and people involved in the story, paying attention as much to nonverbal as verbal cues.

- Performing a kind of social autopsy wherein the reporter paints a scene-by-scene portrait of the setting, people, and events they are involved in.

- Using abundant dialogue, some of which is based on the reporter's informed impressions of what the individual would say, were he or she given the chance to say it in his or her own unique ways.

- Adopting and adapting techniques of fiction writing, such as starting with details that lead to mounting action and climax, followed by a neat and often surprising ending. In short, telling the story in the narrative structure.

- Using a lot of inference and, at times, inventing events or quotes the writer believes would have happened or been said.

An example of this kind of approach can be found in Wolfe's historical look at the U.S. space program: his book called *The Right Stuff*. In one passage, where he recounts NASA releasing the news that monkeys would be making the first space flights, Wolfe says the media reacted to sarcasm from pilot Chuck Yeager as follows:

The press, the eternal gentlemen, just couldn't deal with what he (Chuck Yeager) had said. The wire services wouldn't touch the remark. It ran in one of the local newspapers, and that was that...Here was everybody talking as if the Mercury astronauts would be the first men to ride rockets. Yeager had done precisely that more than forty times. Fifteen other pilots had done it also, and they had reached speeds greater than three times the speed of sound...and that was just the beginning. All of this should have been absolutely obvious to anyone, even people who knew nothing about flying—and surely it would become clear that anybody in Project Mercury was more of a test subject than a pilot.[4]

In another passage, Wolfe describes the scene in which the original Mercury Seven astronaut team is introduced to the giddy and bedazzled press for the first time:

With that, applause erupted, applause of the most fervent sort, amazing applause. Reporters rose to their feet, applauding as if they had come for no other reason. Smiles of weepy and grateful sympathy washed across their faces. They gulped, they cheered, as if this were one of the most inspiring moments of their lives. Even some of the photographers straightened up from out of their beggar's crouches and let their cameras dangle from their straps, so that they could use their hands for clapping. But for what?[5]

Critics of this approach ask a simple question about its validity: "Where is the baseline of documentation?" If it is found in a reporter's impression of what is happening or of what a person is like, it's not very hard documentation, they say. Supporters of the approach ask what's so wrong with trusting a trained observer to deliver a valid portrayal of the scene in front of him?

## The Investigative Approach

To some journalists, all reporting is investigative reporting. It all involves research, digging, interviewing, and divining the truth. But purists insist that true investigative reporting is different from daily deadline reporting. It often involves a reporter or team being assigned to one story for a very long period of time. So Donald Barlett and James Steele of the *Philadelphia Inquirer* spent an enormous amount of time researching an investigative series about America's shrinking middle class called, "America: What Went Wrong?" This series was an analysis of how the rulemakers in Washington and the dealmakers on Wall Street have changed the rules of the game to favor the privileged, the powerful, and the influential—at the expense of everyone else. The series was the culmination of two years of research by these two intrepid journalists.

A similar example of investigative reporting came from a team of reporters from *The Indianapolis Star* who spent a year researching and reporting a series on medical malpractice in the State of Indiana. Both efforts won Pulitzer Prizes.

The investigative approach was popularized in the 1970s by the *Washington Post's* Bob Woodward and Carl Bernstein in their Watergate series of stories. The approach takes a lot of time, a fair amount of talent, and a lot of money especially when a newspaper factors in taking a reporter or two out of the daily production of stories. It also involves prying open stories that people are trying to keep tightly sealed. Investigative reporters often must go through the laborious—and sometimes exasperating—process of filing Freedom of Information requests with the federal government or getting state attorney general support for prying open state or local records.

An even more difficult part of investigative reporting sometimes involves the ethics of reporting tactics themselves. The issue of ends versus means often crops up when a reporter is trying to obtain candor and truth from individuals, agencies, or organizations that are threatened by the truth. Woodward and Bernstein themselves came perilously close to a contempt-of-court citation for some of their efforts to interview grand jury members in the course of their Watergate reporting. But in other ways, investigative reporters must ask themselves about the means they are using to get stories. Often they are asking innocent people, who must risk a lot, to open up and tell what they know about malfeasance or corruption they've witnessed. Such was the case with the CBS *60 Minutes* investigative story on Brown and Williamson Tobacco Company. In that story, producer Lowell Bergman had to find ways to get Dr. Jeffrey Wigand to blow the whistle on Brown and Williamson's spiking of their cigarettes to provide an added addictive nicotine boost for smokers. In this case, although Wigand wanted to tell the story, the personal consequences to him were staggering at times. So Bergman had to find a balanced way of dealing with his source, wanting him to come forward, believing it was a hugely important story for America, but at the same time understanding Wigand's hesitancy at times.

One major trick for investigative reporters is to remain balanced themselves in their approach; to remain highly skeptical while not crossing the line into cynicism. It is a matter of questioning everything while not adopting an *a priori* or advance position that you are going to be lied to or misled by those you interview. An early twentieth century investigative journalist ("muckrakers" as Theodore Roosevelt dubbed them) was Lincoln Steffens, reporter of the famed "Shame of the Cities" series, which appeared in the pages of *McClure's* magazine early in the twentieth century. Steffens had a belief that what was apparent, when it came to city government anyway, was not what was real. He believed that in all cases there was a certain amount of corruption present, and that there always lurked behind the façade, a more invisible hand that directed the activities of the government for private good. So he took on some of the major cities such as St. Louis and Chicago, often successfully proving his theory. At least as it applied to the management of these cities. Biographers report that Steffens died an unhappy man, cynical about life in general and in doubt about the truth.

Always dangerous for any reporter is taking an *a priori* opinion into any story. Always must the facts gleaned by the reporter speak for themselves, and only after that should they speak. It is a lesson all college students learn when they turn in a term paper that is driven by a priori reasoning or conclusions instead of one in which the conclusions follow the evidence researched. In this respect, cynicism can be as bad—or worse in some cases—than its counterpart, naivety.

Before leaving the Investigative orientation, let's talk a minute about something that is often linked with investigative reporting: the practice of deception by journalists to get the story. Investigative reporting is not always done using deception, but often it does entail some form of it because investigative reporters are usually trying to expose a story that someone is working hard to cover up. Journalists are misled, lied to, and deceived themselves by sources, so many feel they must react accordingly to level the reporting playing field. This practice of deception has drawn the ire of some critics, both nonjournalists and journalists alike. A firestorm was created, for instance, when writer Janet Malcolm unleashed a two-part diatribe against journalists in the March 13 and 20, 1989, editions of the *New Yorker* magazine, which later became a book called, "The Journalist and the Murderer." Some of her most scathing criticism of journalists comes in the opening sentences of the article.

Every journalist who is not too stupid or too full of himself to notice what is going on knows that what he does is morally indefensible. He is a kind of confidence man, preying on people's vanity, ignorance, or loneliness, gaining their trust and betraying them without remorse.[6]

Although this was written in 1989, it is still being cited today by critics of the media. For example, Timothy McVeigh's former lead attorney, Stephen Jones, began his remarks in a series of lectures in November 2001 to University of Memphis students by citing that very passage as proof that journalists engage freely in deception.

Malcolm's attack unleashed a barrage of reactions from some respected journalists. Most criticized the sweep of her accusations, yet also agreed that reporter/source relationships pose several problems. Some of the reactions were as follows:[7]

As a journalist, you do some role playing. You don't turn all your cards face up...(But) in a sense it's pointless to try to make distinctions between seduction and persuasion or urging or whatever. In each case what you're trying to do is get cooperation.—*Mike Wallace.*

Those ivory-tower arguments of Malcolm's were just so much crap to me. That opening sentence just blew me away. If anything, I think many of the people I have interviewed as a policeman and as a journalist were trying to con me all the time. I never felt that I was conning anybody.—*Joseph Wambaugh.*

There can scarcely be a reporter, a writer, an editor...who is not arrested by Malcolm's startling opening sentence. I must say, however, that the beginning seems to me to be a profoundly silly one. I am certainly not denying that reporters do their share of manipulation. Of course they do. But the relationship is mutually manipulative.—*J. Anthony Lucas.*

One of the most recent examples of deception in investigative reporting came when journalists for ABC's *Prime Time Live* passed themselves off as job candidates for a Food Lion supermarket, were hired, and spent time documenting—by way of hidden cameras—improper meat-packaging procedures and other consumer abuses. Food Lion took ABC to court, not on the basis of libel but on charges of fraud, and won the case. A jury awarded them a multi-million-dollar judgment. ABC appealed the case to the Supreme Court, which admitted fraud did occur when the journalists posed as store employees and were paid by Food Lion, but the Justices also reduced the amount of the judgment to totally insignificant amounts. The press hailed the decision as a victory.

Deception is a hotly debated issue at many news organizations, and many editors only allow undercover reporting to take place as a last resort, when all other attempts at finding the truth of a significant story fail.

The next perspective discussed talks about the importance of a reporter's doing his or her homework before crafting the story.

## The Friendly Eye Approach

To some degree, you might find this approach at 180-degree odds with the Investigative Approach. On the other hand, looking more closely, there is a lot of similarity between them, especially in the degree of intensive research called for. This perspective, as typified by such journalists as William Dean Howells, believes that—on balance—the kindlier view of man is apt to be the truer view. Also, possibly more than the other approaches discussed, it posits the journalist must do exhaustive homework on an individual before he or she portrays them in a certain definitive way. Howells believed, for instance, that journalists should not judge a person by the way that person responds to a crisis situation. Instead, he advised, look at the person's life steadily and wholly before categorizing him.

Howells, a former editor of *Atlantic Monthly* magazine, was a journalist in the so-called Age of Realism in the early twentieth century. It was a time when Ida M. Tarbell was exposing malfeasance with her "History of the Standard Oil Company," when Steffens was writing his "Shame of the Cities," (both for *McClure's* magazine) and Samuel Hopkins Adams was reporting "The Great American Fraud," for *Collier's*, digging into the patent-medicine business. It was a no-nonsense time of crusading journalism and bursting the bubble many businesses were using to distract the public from their corrupt dealings. Howells was a part of this Age of Realism in writing, and he said he was not suggesting that reporters sugar-coat the truth or present personalities in a false light. He simply suggested that realism often emerges from "seeing life steadily and seeing it wholly," and that when you do your homework on the sweep of a person's life and contributions, you will generally find a more positive than negative view of that person.

### The Pseudo Approach

The August 11, 1980, cover of *Time* magazine featured an artist's rendering of television bad guy J. R. Ewing of *Dallas* fame. The single-word headline above the picture was, "WHODUNNIT?" As even casual viewers knew during that summer, this was the big question to be answered come September and the renewal of the mother of evening soap operas would reappear. So it may not be surprising to some that newspapers like the esteemed *St. Louis Post-Dispatch* featured front-page stories on Saturday, September 20 (the morning after the attacker's identity was revealed), letting readers know the culprit was, indeed, Kristin Shepard. The magnitude of this summer-long story and its impact on the average American was amazing.

All this may be fascinating, but what does it have to do with journalism? Just this: the J. R. Ewing saga is a classic example of a shadow passing itself off as substance to millions of Americans. And it did it with the help of the U.S. news media. I even remember reading about a southern church congregation getting so carried away with the drama that they actually prayed for the soul of J. R., should he die.

Daniel J. Boorstin, librarian-emeritus of Congress, refers to this type of sensation-seeking reporting as "pseudo-journalism."[8] It comes from the knowledge reporters have that Americans are yearning for the image, Boorstin says: for something more bizarre, more exciting than people think they can experience in reality. The problem is that the news media, in their race to lure readers and viewers, are serving up too much of that image to the neglect of more serious and substantive stories. The focus is often more on pseudo-events than real events.

What is a pseudo-event? Briefly, it is an event that is designed to be dramatic, and, therefore, features more flash than substance. It is a planned event, as opposed to spontaneous, and it has little significance on the lives of readers or viewers. In fact, the only impact many of these events or characters have on the public is a titillating one, making them laugh, or utter an omigosh! The problem is this is a manipulated omigosh, and it is outside the arena of real news and inside the arena of public relations and/or sales itself.

To say the news media do not serve an entertainment function is naïve and foolhardy. It is one function journalists and their stories fulfill, but in the case of newspapers anyway or serious television news, it should not be the dominant function as it is becoming at some news organizations. As long as everyone recognizes this is designed to entertain and not to inform or present a picture of reality, there is little harm in it unless pseudonews greatly reduces the news hole for more legitimate stories that do deliver a slice of reality that impacts readers and viewers' lives. Where reporters too often fall prey to pseudo-journalism, however, is not in chasing the J.R. Ewing stories but in chasing subtler events and lower-profile personalities who try to disguise staged actions or press conferences of their own or of their clients as newsworthy. On many occasions reporters have been made to look foolish by their overreliance on news coming from a press conference as being legitimate. A sobering picture of how much the media rely on routine channels of information was portrayed in a study that found more than half the stories in researched editions of the *New York Times* and the *Washington Post* (as well as more than two-thirds of all wire stories) came through routine channels of information like press conferences, press releases, and official proceedings.[9]

Another kind of pseudo-approach to journalism is that represented by the group of journalists/celebrities/entertainers who often pass back and forth across these boundaries with abandon. Certainly daytime television and radio talk shows are replete with these people who appear to be journalists in that they ask questions, deal with controversial issues, and often interview celebrities. But the ways in which they do this, the kinds of issues they focus on, and the intent of what they do often separates them from more legitimate or mainstream forms of journalism. Hyping and recreating events with paid actors are often the norm, as are using slow-motion video when showing something particularly graphic or dramatic. Exploitation of people whose only real interest is to be on television is another common tactic, even if it means exposing the most personal and private aspects of their lives to an audience that is tuning in voyeuristically or to give them something to gossip about with others. There is little or no attempt to separate fact from opinion (often the talk show host's), and the whole effort is supervised by entertainment producers and not news people.

## The Village Approach

Sometimes journalism and anthropology don't seem far removed from each other as means of getting at the truth of a society and its people. In broad terms, an anthropologist spends a great deal of time examining a culture through its artifacts and through interviewing surviving members of that culture. In that sense, journalists like Richard Critchfield, mentioned earlier, are journalistic anthropologists. A former newspaperman, Critchfield left the world of daily deadlines to probe deeper into various cultures. And he did it by going out and spending time in the villages of the world—mostly the Third World. In so doing, he produced books that include *The Long Charade*, about Vietnam, and *Those Days*, about rural change in America from the 1880s to World War II. Several years ago, Critchfield described his unique method of village reporting for the *Washington Journalism Review* (now the *American Journalism Review*).

"Since 1969 I have been systematically going out to live in villages as a kind of storytelling amateur anthropologist," Critchfield said. "This work has involved living in a village for weeks, months, and, in three cases, a year spread out over several visits, usually with a locally recruited interpreter."[10]

Critchfield said he follows the participant observer method of modern anthropology, trying to do the same physical work as his village subjects, while his interpreter tries to record stenographically almost everything they say. He gradually feels his way, while taking careful, continual notes, mostly of dialogue, into getting to know individuals and families. When he sits down to write his story, after typing as many as 20 or 30 notebooks, he hopes that in the dialogue he's taken down, the full life and character of a few villagers will emerge. Critchfield believes these villagers are persons whose individuality and destiny appear framed by the setting of the changing culture and technology around them.[11]

In preparation for his journeys to villages, Critchfield reads up on the local politics, geography, economics, and history—as well as the religion—of the people. The cultural views that count, he feels, are those that emerge in the village dialogue.

When I write the story, I allow myself latitude to select scenes and conversations to create a coherent narrative, while keeping to one strict rule: Never invent a word of what people say. (My dialogue) is laboriously gathered through what might be called "selective eavesdropping," except that I am quite open about it...A striking difference between reporting from villages and reporting from Washington, is the degree of stress...In a Village, for long periods of time you do nothing at all but sit. A Western city dweller's mentality is to do; a villager's mentality is often just to be...Common work, common food, common discomforts soon break down any barriers between people.[12]

Why go to all this trouble, when most of the world's foreign correspondency is done from the capitals of the various nations around the world? Journalists like Critchfield believe that reporting from villages is the best way to learn about how other people in the world think and feel. They agree with writer V. S. Naipaul who says that all the trouble in the world comes from the need of all of its people to adapt quite suddenly to the West and its ways; trying to fit in with Western ideas and Western thought. Critchfield continues:

The value of village reporting is that it forces the reporter to look at problems not in terms of the politics Of the surface, as reporters habitually do, but in terms of technological and cultural trends beneath the surface. Because a village is small and simple, not big and complex like a city, it is easier there to see how culture works, how it changes and how this affects the big political stories.[13]

So, according to journalists who follow this approach, if you want to understand the reasons for the rise of the Taliban, you must spend time in an Afghan village, among its people. Or to understand the assassination of Indira Gandhi, you must spend time in a Sikh Punjabi village. Critchfield concludes:

Go out and live in a village...work with the people, share their lives, listen to what they have to say, write it all down and type up your notes. The reality of what you have found will be so plain that the story will practically write itself. When you look at the world this way it becomes a vast, ongoing, revolutionary drama in perpetual movement, In which countless individual actors—the villagers and city slum dwellers alike—are making choices and taking actions to learn, adapt, grow, and survive.[14]

Critics of this approach might well be the same ones as those criticizing the approach of George Plimpton, discussed earlier. Actually these two orientations are very similar in their participative approach by the journalists covering the stories. How easy is it, a critic would ask, to retain your objectivity about a group of people and their lives when you are immersing yourselves so much in their culture and befriending them? Proponents of these approaches, however, would argue that what you might give up in objectivity, you more than make up for in depth of understanding of the people and their culture.

This approach is closely aligned with the social researcher's participant observation method. It has been used for decades by journalists. For example:

- Nellie Bly of the *New York World* faked insanity to go inside an asylum for the insane in the 1880s and report on conditions as they really existed there.
- A St. Louis television reporter for the ABC affiliate in 1982 moved onto the streets for a month to see what it was like to live on nothing but a social security check.
- Mike Keller of the *Honolulu Advertiser* spent almost a week in the State Prison of Hawaii in the company of hardened criminals to write an eight-part series on the challenges inmates experience in living behind bars.
- ABC's *Prime Time Live* sent undercover investigators inside the Food Lion Supermarket chain in the late 1990s to secretly record food-packaging abuses.

And the list goes on and on. In fact, participative observation has become aligned with investigative journalism in several instances. In its purer form, as Critchfield practices it, however, it is simply the practice of living with the natives to depict an accurate picture of their lives and environment. Writing in the book *Advanced Reporting: Beyond News Events*, Gerry Keir, Maxwell McCombs and Donald Shaw write:

Participant observation enables you to work in situations where the overt presence of a journalist could change people's behavior...The journalist's goal is to describe normal times, not an artificial reality constructed for the benefit of a reporter...Participant observation frees the journalist from relying solely on "official" versions of the truth. It's one thing for a nursing home supervisor to tell you that bedridden patients are bathed every second day. It's quite another to see for yourself as an orderly that once a week is the rule.[15]

The authors suggest the following guidelines for effective participant observation:

- Make your hypotheses up as you go along. Normally you don't enter a situation seeking to prove or disprove a particular hypothesis. You discover the rules of the game as you watch it and participate in it.
- Give yourself enough time to understand things.
- Make complete notes on what you observe as soon as possible after observing it.
- Don't take sides. Position yourself socially so you can communicate with all factions.
- Pay attention to how other people around you view the world. You are there to see how reality is perceived by others; not to impose your theories of reality upon them.
- When you are finished, you do not have numbers to analyze and discuss. You have a series of qualitative impressions instead.

- Be prepared to spend time and money.
- The logistical problems of living with your subjects are many. You need considerable advance planning if you are to succeed. There also may be ethical reasons that prevent you from gathering information through deception.[16]

As in other approaches to journalism, this one will only be successful in presenting an accurate picture of your subjects if you stay neutral, even while living among the villagers.

## The Economic Perspective

The approaches that have been discussed so far all have one thing in common: they are predicated on presenting an accurate view of the world because that is what the journalism profession mandates and what readers and viewers need. The approach I call the Economic Perspective is not necessarily restricted by this ideal. In one sense, it is a kind of amoral perspective insofar as it is not driven by journalistic ideology or zeal. It is instead driven by the bottom line, and the journalism that results is meant to enhance that bottom line through higher readership or viewership. The choice of stories, as well as their construction, are based on marketing considerations much more than pure news value criteria. Indeed, the decision of whether to really *do* news reporting is a decision that some major media companies are wrestling with as of this writing. A classic example is the debate surrounding whether the Disney Company, owners of ABC Television, think it is feasible to stay in the news business—at least to the degree the network has been involved in it. In the spring of 2002 the debate focused on whether to keep the highly respected *Nightline* program or jettison it in favor of a late-night comedian.

In fact, David Letterman reportedly turned down a lucrative offer from ABC to jump ship at CBS and switch networks. Letterman had made it known he would not move if it meant dislodging newsman Ted Koppel or his *Nightline* from ABC. To the executives of Disney, however, this whole thing was a business decision whose goal was to right the corporate ship of ABC, which was faltering in the ratings and in revenues at the time. Executives were quoted as saying they wouldn't let sentimental attachment to an aging news program stand in their way of righting the corporate ship.

The Economic Perspective reminds us that news is, in addition to being a public service, first and foremost a business for those underwriting the costs of producing it. And it has been that way since the age of the so-called penny press in the 1830s when publishers like James Gordon Bennett realized how popular a commodity news could be with the average American, especially if presented in the right way. As in any of the perspectives or approaches discussed in this chapter, followers of the Economic Perspective are arrayed upon a scale of making news decisions solely on the basis of anticipated revenue, to those who would temper moneymaking with the goals, nature, and ideals of journalism as a public service.

The consequences of this economic approach to journalism have been the subject of much discussion in the professional media reviews as well as academic journals over the past three decades. In particular, publicly traded media companies have been scrutinized for changes in their editorial philosophy over the years. For example, a 1993 research study by Blankenberg and Ozanich discovered that public media companies put more emphasis on profits and are more attuned to investors than private companies. They also discovered that public media companies are more interested in short-term returns than long-term investments. The researchers concluded:

The results support the notion that local newspaper owners may be in the business to achieve other goals besides maximizing profits...Maybe traditional newspaper owners...have non-monetary motivations such as prestige and satisfaction from performing a public service.[17]

And an analysis of one high-profile public media company found in the early 1990s:

It is important to note that a schism exists between the financial and editorial/readership needs of the papers. Rather than adhering to decisions to increase readership as the means to obtain healthy returns on revenue, operating decisions have ultimately led to cost-cutting to enhance revenue...When owned by (the previous owners), this company's operating environment supported an emphasis on editorial excellence that created readership which, in turn, created revenue. When (joined with the current ownership) the new owners had to address changing business, economic and social conditions. (The company's) focus has been on short-term financial results to ensure financial viability. This has led to cutting costs to enhance revenue, which has resulted in frequently changing and often abandoned initiatives to gain greater readership.[18]

Certainly the Economic Perspective goes far beyond the approach an individual journalist might take—or prefer to take—in covering a story. It goes to management policies and the philosophy of the company for which she works. But those policies, as all journalists know, directly affect what the reporter has a chance to cover and how much time can be spent on the project.

## The Virtual Perspective

Where does a journalist draw the line between what really happened and a representation of what really happened? And when does a story enter into the realm of hype or overwriting in order to make a point, and is that legitimate journalism? In an article entitled, "Spicing up the (ho-hum) truth," John Leo raises the issues and points to a couple examples including the following:[19]

On January 4, 1993, *NBC Nightly News* showed some powerful pictures of how clear-cutting by the timber industry was fouling streams and killing fish in the Clearwater National Forest in Idaho. The problem is that NBC learned later the dead fish weren't from Clearwater, and the Clearwater fish weren't dead.

Another case in point, this one more familiar: *Dateline NBC* rigged a GM pickup to explode helpfully on camera to represent how other GM pickups were behaving if hit in the right spot, at the right time. The problem is, *Dateline* didn't bother to tell viewers the event was staged. Corporate heads rolled over that mistake.

And a third example: *USA Today* suspended a reporter for staging a front-page photo of ominous gun-bearing gang members. The young men had been sent home to get their guns to pose for the picture.

Even PBS hasn't been immune from this Virtual Approach to journalism. A PBS documentary on how black troops fed Jews from Dachau and Buchenwald was pulled for review when news broke that some members of the black regiment involved said they had never been anywhere near either camp.

Questioning whether such reporting might represent not just a lapse in accuracy but an intentional deception to hype the drama of the aired story, Leo asks:

But what if it wasn't a lapse? What if it was a preview of what news is destined to become, as images, story line and emotional impact begin to erode the old commitment to literal truth?[20]

He goes on to quote Richard Reeves, a syndicated columnist with good contacts in television who explicitly makes this argument, saying the "old guard has disappeared from television news, and the business is now in the hands of a new generation whose members don't think of themselves as reporters or producers, but as filmmakers, with little interest in words and heavy interest in dramatic effect." To Reeves, the GM truck explosions were a watershed event.[21]

In another essay, five years later, Leo makes a similar case in an article entitled, "Nothing but the truth?" In this essay he looks at the cases of high-profile journalists like Patricia Smith of the *Boston Globe,* and Stephen Glass of the *New Republic* who were both caught lying in print. The *New Republic* discovered that Glass had made up all or part of at least 27 of 41 articles in the magazine over a 30-month period. Leo notes:

The 20-something Glass made a name for himself quickly partly because of his output (huge) but mostly because of the startling stories he turned up that nobody else seemed to have. One of the most memorable was the tale of drunken young conservatives humiliating a homeless woman at a Washington hotel...Glass is an extreme case. He filled notebooks with phantom interviews and even created an Internet Web site to document one of his fictional stories.[22]

For her part, columnist Smith was asked by the *Globe* to resign after admitting she made up parts of four recent columns. A finalist for the 1989 Pulitzer Prize for commentary, Smith told dramatic and emotional stories of everyday life in the Boston area. For example, she acknowledged fabricating almost completely a column about Claire, a woman dying of cancer, and a man named Jim Burke, a worker putting up barricades at the Boston Marathon.

In her apology to readers, Smith wrote:

I wanted the pieces to jolt, to be talked about, to leave the readers indelibly impressed...I will survive this knowing that the heart of my columns was honest and heartfelt.[23]

In responding to Smith's letter, Tom Rosenstiel of the Project for Excellence in Journalism makes an interesting point: "You get the sense reading her apology that she has the mentality of an artist who's talking about the truth with a capital T. But journalism is fundamentally about nonfiction."[24] Others might ask, however: Why must the two be so different?

### The Advocacy Perspective

A central tenet of traditional journalism is the notion of objectivity; of the reporter remaining neutral on issues and people and telling both sides of the story. It is so ingrained in beginning journalists that it seems obvious that good journalism equals objective journalism. It might come as something of a surprise, however, to discover that not all mainstream journalists feel that way. For some, there are issues or causes for which there is no legitimate other side.

For example, a lot of journalists would say there is no other side to torture or brutal slayings. Or they might say there is no other side to wanton destruction of innocent lives, such as in the cases of the Twin Towers or the Oklahoma City bombing. During the Vietnam War, some journalists crossed the line of objectivity by stating the United States had no business being in Vietnam. Indeed, CBS news anchor Walter Cronkite, once viewed by many as the most respected journalist in America, pronounced the Vietnam War unable to be won, following his return from the battlefield. Some journalists believe there is no other side to nuclear destruction or possessing the capabilities to produce nuclear holocaust. And others believe there is no other side to the environmental issue; that it is imperative the federal government conserve natural resources and protect endangered species.

During the 1960s and early 1970s, advocacy journalism seemed to reach its zenith as alternative or underground newspapers arose in cities from Berkeley, Calif., to New York City. These papers, like the *Berkeley Barb*, exhorted citizens to put pressure on the government to get American troops out of Vietnam. Lauren Kessler, in her book *The Dissident Press*, cites some of these antiwar newspapers including the *National Guardian*, founded by two professional newspapermen who promoted the Progressive Party candidate Henry Wallace for president.

From its inception, the *Guardian* began covering the developments in Vietnam, reporting on the postwar betrayal of the French and the defeat of the French Army. With a peak of circulation of 100,000 and subscribers in small towns from Arkansas to Oregon—in addition to the traditional urban leftist audience—the *Guardian* was one of the few sources of independent (nongovernment) information about the war...By mid-1963 the *National Guardian* was calling Vietnam, "The Dirty War"..."The Handwriting is on the wall for the U.S. misadventure in Vietnam," wrote *Guardian* editor James Aronson in early 1964. "The struggle may be long drawn, but this is a war the United States cannot win."[25]

Kessler cites *Ramparts*, a small-circulation intellectual Catholic magazine that in 1965 became a popular leftist monthly, as another important antiwar voice. In the 1960s its circulation rose to 250,000. She notes, "*Ramparts* was the first popular periodical to reveal the extent and the premeditation of U.S. involvement in Vietnam."[26]

These and other leftist publications also called for various civil rights reforms and some of them often championed the legalization of marijuana. That was advocacy journalism in its extreme form, but shades of it are still with us today.

As chapter 1 discussed, not all journalists are unified on how environmental reporters should orient themselves to their craft. Many believe the environmental beat should be handled no differently from any other, but others disagree. These journalists believe environmental reporters should assume the role of advocates or protectors of a clean and safe environment. They feel part of their role is to make sure the government notices the problems and takes steps to solve them.

The environmental advocacy point of view is possibly best summed up by Dr. Michael Frome, former conservation editor of *Field and Stream*, columnist for the *Los Angeles Times*, and author of several books on the environment. Frome believes the motivation should be to show the intangible values of the human heart and spirit and how living in harmony with nature can only lead to living in harmony with each other.[27] Frome points to journalists like the late Ed Meeman of the old *Memphis Press-*

*Scimitar,* who made conservation a front-page story and who crusades for creation of the Great Smoky Mountains National Park. Frome says:

The environmental journalist begins with hope that things can be better. We must reawaken the environmental consciousness we all inherit. The inverted pyramid is not enough. The environmental journalist looks at the whole, examining all the interlocking aspects of life from politics, to religion, to ecology. The environmental journalists should be like a scientist while writing independently, letting the chips fall where they may, with consequences to follow. I just found a lot of bastards screwing up the environment. A journalist's job is to expose the bastards. We need to get some good advocates and journalists to shake up the place. But I consider myself a journalist First. Environmentalism is my specialty. The issues are what fire my belly. Journalism is my way of venting that fire.[28]

Before leaving this section, it is interesting to note some other more subtle forms this advocacy debate among journalists often takes. In covering the Oklahoma City bombing and its aftermath in the spring of 1995, many journalists at Ground Zero chose to wear blue, white, and yellow ribbons in memory of the innocent dead in and around the Alfred C. Murrah Building. Others chose not to wear the ribbons and said nothing about the issue. Still others chose not to wear the ribbons and were vocal in their opposition of those reporters who did, saying, "Journalists aren't supposed to take sides." The question is whether showing support for surviving relatives and memorializing the dead is really taking sides or not. Journalists wearing the ribbons might well say that caring about innocent deaths and mass destruction doesn't mean they are any less objective in reporting what happened and why it did. And it certainly doesn't follow that they are taking the side of the governmental officials or given to just reporting the official story.

The same debate arose with reporters wearing ribbons or American flags in their lapel in the aftermath of the Jonesboro, Ark., school shootings, and in the coverage of the Twin Towers bombing. That's how sensitive some reporters are about the unique role journalists occupy.

## The Larger Truth Perspective

In 1938, the first edition of what came to be a classic reporting textbook appeared. It was called, *Interpretive Reporting,* and it was written by Curtis D. MacDougall. In it, the author broke with traditionalists who had been saying for years that the job of the reporter is to tell the "what," and not so much the "why" of a story. To many traditionalists of the day, plunging into the "why" was putting a reporter at risk in taking him or her into the world of subjectivity; of interpretation. MacDougall disagreed. In the fourth edition of his book, he writes about the need for interpretive reporting:

The successful journalist of the future...must be capable of more than routine coverage and interpret as well as report what is going on. To interpret the news it is necessary to understand it, and understanding means more than just the ability to define the jargon used by persons in different walks of life. It involves recognizing the particular event as one of a series with both a cause and effect. With their perspective the historians of the future may be better able to depict the trends and currents of the present...(The journalist) will at least be aware of the fact that news is not an isolated incident but one inevitably linked to a chain of important events.[29]

MacDougall concludes, "The best stories are not generally found near the surface. Only the reporter who cultivates the habit of constant, thorough thoughtfulness finds them."[30]

While some critics of interpretive reporting still seem to confuse interpretation with editorializing or making value judgments, others simply see interpretation as the inevitable process of reporting. To them, interpretation and reporting are inseparable. Journalist and researcher William Rivers has noted for example:

The link between fact and interpretation is even broader. The American Heritage Dictionary defines fact as "1. Something known with certainty. 2. Something asserted as certain." It is a fact that Mickey Rooney is short. But this is actually an interpretation derived from comparison. To a Pygmy in the Ituri Forest of Zaire, Rooney would be a towering figure. So it is with most facts—the "data" of the historian or the social scientist as well as the experiences of daily life. They are relative and must be interpreted in the light of other facts. In short, there is seldom a real distinction between gathering facts and expressing ideas. As someone once said, "most of the facts we gather come dripping with ideas."[31]

With interpretation comes the attempt to go beyond individual facts and treat them like pieces of a jigsaw puzzle, connecting the right ones together until you have the completed puzzle solved. Until you have the full, larger picture. But some writers balk at journalism pursuing the larger truth and say that is not really the business of the deadline reporter. One such critic of journalists as pursuers of the larger truth is Roger Rosenblatt who once wrote:

When journalists hear journalists claim a "larger truth," they really ought to go for their pistols...The business of journalism is to present facts accurately. Those seeking something larger are advised to look elsewhere. For one thing, journalism rarely sees the larger truth of a story because reporters are usually chasing quite small elements of information. A story, like a fern, only reveals its final, shocking shape in stages...If one asks, then, where the larger truth is to be sought, the answer is where it has always been: in history, conversation; in the tunnels of one's own mind. People may have come to expect too much of journalism.[32]

Other media reviewers, like Gerry Keir, Maxwell McCombs, and Donald L. Shaw, defend the presentation of the larger truth, however, and decry what they see as superficial, event-oriented reporting that presents incidents as isolated and somehow disconnected from larger patterns or underlying currents. They call upon journalists to present more of a "social mosaic," pulling the individual tiles together to form a larger, more complete picture by reporting systematically with the use of the tools of the social scientist such as surveys, content analysis, and even participant observation.[33]

In defense of this larger-picture reporting, former *New York Daily News* Editor Mike O'Neill once said, "We need to put more emphasis on what I call preventive journalism—deliberately searching for the underlying social currents that threaten future danger so that public policy can be more intelligently mobilized."[34]

Critics of this approach point out that event-oriented and personality-driven stories are the ones that most interest readers, whose attention spans are relatively short. Issue-oriented stories—depth reporting—might win journalistic awards, but they doesn't necessarily win readers or viewers. One thinks of a scene in the Peter Weir film, *The Year of Living Dangerously,* mentioned earlier. Reporter Guy Hamilton is befriended by a multiethnic photojournalist named Billy Kwan (more insightful but also somewhat of an advocate journalist) who tries to get him to tell the story of the people of Indonesia in the early 1960s and how they are suffering under the Sukarno regime. The young Hamilton rejects the idea saying, "No one will listen. They don't want to hear it." Kwan replies simply, "Tell them anyway."

### The Storyteller Perspective

Once the purview of creative writers who deal in fiction, now storytelling has been adapted to—and adopted by—the journalistic community en masse. This concept of fitting the narrative structure—or at least large chunks of it—to journalistic style has had a profound effect on the orientation of many journalists. It is a concept that goes beyond mere story structure, of using say an hourglass format rather than the inverted pyramid. It goes to the way journalists approach stories, who they talk to, and the kind of observations and notes they take. Journalists following the Storytelling Perspective will put more emphasis on the human element of the story, often focusing it on one or just a few individuals who they will then flesh out in the narrative. It is building a story from the ground up, or the inside out, anecdote by anecdote. Despite the name of this perspective, storytelling is the art of *showing* the reader the story, rather than telling it. And you show by fleshing out the key characters, making them human, and showing them in action.

Suffice it to say here that storytelling can incorporate any of the perspectives previously discussed, depending on the kind of story being done. But the result is a story that should grab the reader, pull her in, and cause her to identify with or care about the characters and issues involved. It is the perspective that some recent authors have used in creating best-selling nonfiction books. Most notably is Sebastian Junger, author of *The Perfect Storm*, which features many gripping passages like the following:

A soft rain slips down through the trees, and the smell of ocean is so strong it can almost be licked off the air...the ocean swells up against the black pilings and sucks back down to the barnacles.[35]

And this:

For a brief while, it's possible to surf across people's lawns...by nightfall, the ocean is two feet deep in some of the nicest living rooms of the state.[36]

In describing his approach, Junger commented in the book, "I wanted to write a completely factual book that would stand on its own as a piece of journalism. (But) I didn't want the narrative to asphyxiate under a mass of technical detail and conjecture."[37]

Adapting this storytelling approach to journalism is not all that new, although it continues to evolve in form and principles. The writer Tom Wolfe is well-known for introducing this kind of literary journalism to the profession in the 1960s and 1970s. But Wolfe's storytelling was critiqued for not sticking strictly to the dialogue that was spoken and for venturing into the territory of what was probably said or what would have been said in this or that situation. It is a kind of literary license that many journalists still have problems with. The difference with Junger's storytelling, at least in the case of *The Perfect Storm*, is he said he followed one cardinal rule: Never invent a word of dialogue. If he was unsure of the actual dialogue of the Andrea Gail's crew members (none of whom survived the ordeal) he would indicate that in the text. To the end of presenting an accurate account of what actually happened and what these people were like who lived the tragedy, Junger did consider himself very much a journalist.

## SUMMARY

The list of different perspectives, orientations, or approaches journalists take into their work will continue to evolve as the creativity of the writers themselves evolves. Some journalists are gifted at practicing several of the perspectives presented in this chapter with equal ease. Others wouldn't know how to fight their way out of the approach or structure they have used their entire career. Still others wouldn't even want to. But part of the beauty and effectiveness of journalism is that the stories journalists produce do evidence such a variety of perspectives and orientations. Since there is so much written about every news event or individual worthy of attention these days, readers and viewers have the opportunity to view—simultaneously if they wish—different approaches or orientations to the same story or the same individual or celebrity. If nothing else, this chapter should destroy the stereotype that some people have of journalists; who think of only one type of individual who does the work of reporting. As is the nature of journalists themselves, this is a profession of individuals who often disagree on a lot of things relating to their work, but who also try to honor the basic tenets of accuracy and fair play.

## NOTES

1. Roger Rosenblatt, "Journalism and the Larger Truth," *Time*, 2 July 1984, 88.

2. Philip Meyer, *The New Precision Journalism* (Bloomington: Indiana University Press, 1991), 3–4.

3. Gerry Keir, Maxwell McCombs, and Donald Shaw, *Advanced Reporting: Beyond News Events* (Prospect Heights, Ill.: Waveland Press, 1991), pp. 231–234.

4. Tom Wolfe, *The Right Stuff* (New York: Bantam Books, 1984), p. 128.

5. Wolfe, 184.

6. Janet Malcolm, *The Journalist and the Murderer* (New York: Vintage Books, 1990), 3.

7. Martin Gottlieb, "Dangerous Liaisons: Journalists and Their Sources," *Columbia Journalism Review* (July/August 1989): 21.

8. Daniel J. Boorstin, *The Image: A Guide to Pseudo-Events in America* (New York: Atheneum Books, 1985), 9–10.

9. Content analysis of *Washington Post* and *New York Times* on routine news sources.

10. Richard Critchfield, "The Village Voice of Richard Critchfield: Bringing the Third World to the Fourth Estate," *Washington Journalism Review* (October 1985): 27–28.

11. Ibid.

12. Ibid.

13. Ibid.

14. Ibid.

15. Keir, McCombs, and Shaw, 242–244.

16. Ibid.

17. Study by Blankenberg and Ozanich on public media company profits.

18. Ibid.

19. John Leo, "Spicing Up the Ho-Hum Truth," *U.S. News & World Report* (8 March 1993): 24.

20. Ibid.

21. Ibid.

22. John Leo, "Nothing But the Truth?" *U.S. News & World Report* (19 January 1998): 26.

23. Ibid.

24. Ibid.

25. Lauren Kessler, *The Dissident Press: Alternative Journalism in American History* (Beverly Hills: Sage, 1984), 148–149.

26. Ibid.

27. Michael Frome, "Let the Presses Roll Green!" (speech at the University of Memphis, Memphis, Tenn., 17 April 1996).

28. Ibid.

29. Curtis D. MacDougall, *Interpretive Reporting,* 4th ed. (New York: Macmillan, 1963), 14.

30. Ibid.

31. William Rivers, *Finding Facts: Interviewing, Observing, Using Reference Sources* (Englewood Cliffs, N.J.: Prentice-Hall, 1975), 4.

32. Rosenblatt, 88.

33. Keir, McCombs, and Shaw, 25ff.

34. Mike O'Neill, as quoted in Keir, McCombs, and Shaw, 7.

35. Sebastian Junger, *The Perfect Storm* (New York: HarperCollins, 1997), 5.

36. Ibid., 204.

37. Ibid., ix.

# Chapter 3

# Objectivity and Subjectivity

Most people live in a common-sense world, in which the meaning of things, of facts and relations, is taken for granted and self-evident. But could it be that the way they see things is also affected by the threefold prior processes of socialization? Primary socialization leads into a specific culture and sub-culture. Secondary socialization leads into a professional subculture, with all its dos and don'ts. Tertiary socialization leads into a specific organization, with larger patterns, over which he or she has only limited control. And (is) that conformity furthermore subtly regulated by occupational values and peer groups?[1]

Jaap van Ginneken, *Understanding Global News: A Critical Introduction*

In his important study of international journalism, Jaap van Ginneken asks this opening question about journalists and their overall orientation to observation and reporting the news. As many others before him have noted, while objectivity may be a theoretical hallmark of Western journalism (which isn't necessarily shared by the rest of the world's reporting corps), putting it into practice poses great difficulties.

In its strictest definition, an objective observation is one defined by the object itself. An example would be that an emotion would define itself as love or joy. In contrast, a subjective observation is one in which the observer does the defining, based on characteristics of the object as well as characteristics of the observer. It is the latter part of this second definition that often forms the dirty little secret of journalism and one that many reporters don't like to acknowledge. It is often taken for granted that if a reporter does this and that, follows this professional standard or that one (usually involving telling both sides and staying detached from the action and people involved) that objectivity will result. In the strictest sense of the term, however, objectivity is an extreme that can never be realized in the telling of a story unless the object—and not the reporter—tells it itself. And if the object is a human, then the same subjectivity enters in.

As one observer has put it, "Every reporter operates with certain assumptions about what constitutes normative behavior, if not good society, and the more 'objective' he tries to be, the more likely those assumptions will remain concealed."[2] On an international level, as Van Ginneken says, what might appear as "objectivity" to Western audiences (all relevant groups agreeing to the point of view or assumptions in the article), may appear as pure "subjectivity" to non-Western audiences.[3] Take for example a reporter who defines a Palestinian who blows herself and 10 Israelis up a "terrorist," while another reporter might call her a "soldier." One description is based on the assumption that such an act is an unacceptable, unprovoked, and barbaric behavior. The other description sees it as an act of war by a people whose available choice of weapons is limited to human bombs in crowded areas.

It is important to use operational definitions if you want to enhance the validity of objectivity. For example, "terrorism" is a word used a lot these days by people and governments. But does everyone know what distinguishes terrorism from war or from everyday crime? No; so to make sure everyone knew what it was speaking about when using a term in a study, the Rand Corporation developed an operating definition[4] of the term that included the following points:

- Terrorism should be defined by the quality of the act; not the identity of the perpetrator or nature of the cause.
- An act of terrorism is first a crime in the classic sense, albeit one for political motives.
- Terrorists are not "soldiers." Terrorist tactics violate accepted rules of armed conflict.
- The hallmark of terrorism is its intended psychological effect. It is aimed at the people who are watching and not at the people killed.

The concept of objectivity has undergone some major changes just in the evolution of American journalism. In the early stages of mass-circulation dailies of the nineteenth century, "objectivity" first meant a rigorous reporting procedure that was a reaction to—and hopefully antidote to—the sensationalism and jingoism of the press in the nineteenth and early twentieth centuries. For example, when James Gordon Bennett and others brought the daily newspaper into mass popularity in the 1830s and beyond, they often resorted to sensationalism and fiction to reach out and engage the readers. They gave them a good read, and the accuracy of the article was often a secondary consideration. Many readers obviously didn't seem to mind, as circulation of Bennett's *New York Herald*—and later of William Randolph Hearst's *New York Journal*—zoomed into the tens of thousands, and later, the hundreds of thousands.

In the case of Bennett, he was among the first to see the entertainment value in news, and he played it to the hilt. Part of it was his desire to "always be with the people—think with them—feel with them," as he said frequently.[5] He also wrote, "A newspaper can be made to take the lead of all these in the great movements of human thought and of human civilization. A newspaper can send more souls to heaven, and save more from hell, than all the churches or chapels in New York, besides making money at the same time."[6] He believed the newspaper should reflect all of life and relate to the average person on the street. But he also saw the profit value in doing that. As journalism historian Frank Luther Mott put it, "Whether or not he saved any souls by his stories of crime, he certainly made money by them."[7]

Along with the sensationalism came an expanded idea of what journalism should be. Its principles were solid, and the development of the news function meant the hiring of more people specifically devoted to reporting, writing and editing the day's news. Many of the so-called penny papers published their creed from time to time, often with the following points noted:

- The great common people should have a realistic view of the contemporary scene, even in spite of social taboos.
- Abuses in churches, courts, banks, stock markets, and so forth, should be exposed.
- The newspaper's first duty is to give its readers the news, and not to support a party or a mercantile class.
- Local and human-interest news is important.

Along with these principles, however, came the sensationalism. Mott noted, "Bad taste, coarseness which sometimes became indecency, overemphasis on crime and sex, and disreputable advertising were outstanding sins of these papers."[8]

Then there were the infamous hoaxes; the stories invented by reporters out of whole cloth. One such writer of fiction who paraded it as fact was Richard Adams Locke, hired by Benjamin Day to report for the *Sun*. Locke wrote a series of four articles documenting life in space and ending with the sensational tale of "man-bat" inhabitants on the moon. Circulation rose dramatically, even after Locke's moon hoax turned out to be one of the greatest fakes of journalistic history. Even after Locke admitted—albeit over a beer—to a reporter for the rival *Journal of Commerce*, that he had concocted the whole series. Other newspapers turned on the *Sun* with journalistic outrage, but interestingly enough, the public didn't seem to care. Even the *Sun* patted itself on the back for "diverting the public mind, for a while, from that bitter apple of discord, the abolition of slavery."[9]

The apex of the Yellow Journalism Era came in the last decade of the nineteenth century as Joseph Pulitzer and his *New York World* battled it out with William Randolph Hearst and his *New York Journal.* In January 1896 Hearst managed to steal away the entire staff of the successful Sunday edition of Pulitzer's *New York World* simply by offering them more money. A lot more. The battle for circulation in New York City centered on this Sunday edition, widely read by the population of the Big Apple. Heading this Sunday staff was editor Morrill Goddard. It was he who invented the formula for the sensational Sunday paper of the era: a few pages of news an editorial in the normal daily style, plus page spreads or double-pages devoted to exaggerated and sensationalized versions of chosen phases of science or pseudoscience, plus a similar play of some crime material. Add to that some pages of stage comment with emphasis on legs, toss in a sob-sister type of advice column to girls and lover, exploit some prominent literary or social figure (preferably European), add sports, society, and colored supplements of comics, and you have the Sunday formula of the mid-1890s.[10]

Not content to confine his editorial crusades to New York, however, Hearst moved into the international arena in almost single-handedly becoming responsible for America's entry into the Spanish-American War. Here's how it came about: As Pulitzer began tiring of all the yellow journalism, he began placing restrictions on his new Sunday editor, Arthur Brisbane, who was knee-deep in sensationalism. Brisbane was, however, getting the huge sum of $200 a week on the *World*, but was lured away by Hearst for $150 a week with the sum to be increased one dollar for every thousand papers added to the *Journal*'s circulation. The offer would elevate Brisbane's weekly salary to $1,000 weekly during the Spanish-American War.[11] In other words, he added another 850,000 *Journal* readers and was given free hand to be as sensational as he wanted.

As Mott notes, "If Hearst had not challenged Pulitzer to a circulation contest at the time of the Cuban insurrection, there would have been no Spanish-American War. Certainly the most powerful and persistent jingoistic propaganda ever carried on by newspapers was led by the *New York Journal* and *World* in 1896–1898, and the result was an irresistible popular fervor for war which at length overcame the long unwillingness of President McKinley and even swept blindly over the last-minute capitulation by Spain on all the points at issue."[12]

Hearst's *Journal* took the lead in fanning the flames of war passion via news stories, headlines, pictures, and editorials about alleged Spanish atrocities in Cuba. So sure was Hearst that America would enter the fray in Cuba, that he bought a yacht, named the Vamoose, and sent it to Cuba with Richard Harding Davis, famed as a fiction writer, and Frederic Remington, famed as an illustrator. As Mott notes, Remington did not like the assignment and sent a cablegram to Hearst asking to come home. The ensuing exchange of cables read:

HEARST, JOURNAL, NEW YORK:
EVERYTHING IS QUIET. THERE IS NO TROUBLE HERE. THERE WILL BE NO WAR. WISH TO RETURN. REMINGTON.

REMINGTON, HAVANA:
PLEASE REMAIN. YOU FURNISH THE PICTURES AND I'LL FURNISH THE WAR. HEARST.[13]

Finally, late in the evening of February 15, 1898, the United States battleship Maine was blown up by persons unknown while moored in Havana Harbor. Despite the lack of evidence, Hearst offered a $50,000 reward for information leading to the conviction of the culprits, and then proceeded to announce on the front page of the Journal that it was the Spanish Army that had sunk it. Because of the huge circulation of the Journal, that story became a fact accepted by a large percentage of the country, and the war fever was on. Pulitzer's World was not far behind in its efforts to fan the war flames. Again from Mott: "The circulations of both papers again passed the million mark with the news of the destruction of the Maine. Only a war could now keep them on the upward curve."[14]

The War with Spain was ideal for news coverage. In the first place, it was nearby, just 90 miles off the coast of Florida. Also, it was a relatively small war, limited to a confined area, not too hard to cover especially since American commanders gave a free reign to reporters, and it was a short war. Given the public's attention span, even then, and its limited tolerance with the death of its own troops, this was an important factor.

Among the several incidents involving journalists covering this war, none was as fascinating—and revealing of the nature of this kind of participant journalism—as the case of Journal reporter James Creelman. As Louis Snyder and Richard Morris noted, "Some reporters in Cuba wrote the news. James Creelman made the news. His personal exploit at El Caney turned out to be one of the best news stories of the war."[15]

Ironically, it would be a story written by his boss, William Randolph Hearst, who ventured himself to Cuba to tell the tale of his brave reporter. On July 1, 1898, American troops prepared to capture the Spanish blockhouse at El Caney. Creelman, having received an exclusive tip at midnight, slipped away from his colleagues in the press corps and snaked his way to the top of a small hill from where he could see the stone fort at El Caney. Snyder and Morris pick up the story from here:

Crawling forward to an adjacent hill, Creelman caught up with General Chaffee of the American force. Bullets came uncomfortably close. One clipped a button from the general's breast. It seemed better to be shot at fighting than to die watching. The only man to know the back road up the hill, Creelman suggested a bayonet charge and offered to lead the way if Chaffee would send troops to a depression on the hillside where they would be partly sheltered until they were within close rushing distance. Creelman, in the next few moments ceased to be a journalist and found himself a hero.[16]

In his later book containing several of his news reports (*On the Great Highway*, published in 1901), Creelman recalls being wounded in the attack, staggering to a hammock in a small room at the fort, "hearing my own blood drip."[17] He was carried down the hill where he lay among the other wounded soldiers. Then he writes:

Someone knelt in the grass beside me and put his hand on my fevered head. Opening my eyes, I saw Mr. Hearst, the straw hat with a bright ribbon on his head, a revolver at his belt, and a pencil and notebook in his hand. The man who had provoked the war had come to see the result with his own eyes and, finding one of his correspondents prostrate, was doing the work himself. Slowly he took down my story of the fight as he said: "I'm sorry you're hurt, but"—and his face was radiant with enthusiasm— "wasn't it a splendid fight? We must beat every paper in the world."[18]

This was the new and competitive journalistic arena into which a more sobering idea of objectivity took root. In reaction to the obsessions of the so-called yellow press, the banner of fair play was raised high by indignant journalists—as well as other newspaper publishers not making the kind of money that Bennett was over at the *Herald*. In the days that followed, objectivity wasn't just a one-to-one equation with neutrality. It meant more than that. It meant a strict adherence to the facts and a separation from the writer's value statements or opinions. It meant nonfiction instead of fiction.

Later, advocates of objectivity in the 1920s called for journalism based more on the scientific method used by a social scientist. It was felt that humans could not be objective by the very fact that they are human, and that a rigorous procedure like the scientific method was necessary to keep to the facts of the situation. Of course, in the 1920s America had just come out of the experience of World War I in which the nation's press had been effectively recruited by the administration of Woodrow Wilson to convince the country we had to become involved in that war in the first place. Then, once in it, the press dutifully followed the administration's guidelines designed to keep up the American resolve to stay in the war and win it. Walter Lippmann, in his classic essay, "Public Opinion," called it the single most effective effort in history at creating one unified public opinion.[19] And Frank Cobb of the *New York World*, wrote:

For five years there has been no free play of public opinion in the world. Confronted by the inexorable necessities of war, governments conscripted public opinion... they goose-stepped it. They taught it to stand at attention and salute.[20]

So the new idea of objectivity became somewhat of a reaction to this kind of media recruiting or media manipulation by the government. By the way, it was the U.S. government's successful propaganda effort in World War I that paved the way for the start of institutional public relations in America. In any event, this brand of objectivity was heavily influenced by a national skepticism of many journalists in America at the time.

Lippmann, himself a working journalist of great fame, began linking the words "objective," "science," and "scientific" together and became an advocate for adapting the scientific method to journalism as a defense against subconscious or unwarranted opinions creeping into the copy. He, along with psychiatrists like Sigmund Freud, believed that an individual citizen could not intuit truth because he or she is only a creature of his culture. That culture, through its propagandists, could easily play on the emotional nature of journalists as human beings. So the scientific method became Lippmann's way out and his defense mechanism. It was a message that was to be echoed years later—in the 1960s—in the so-called precision journalism approach trumpeted by journalism educators Philip Meyer and later Maxwell McCombs.[21]

Good as it sounded, adapting the scientific method to daily journalism posed many problems. By its nature, the scientific method takes time to develop, and there is no time for daily journalists as the deadline always looms. For newspapers it comes on 24-hour cycles; for television it comes quicker; for today's online journalists, the deadline is instantaneous, 24 hours a day, 60 minutes each hour. Running a content analysis or random-sample survey, interpreting the results, and writing the report takes much longer than the time allotted to most journalists to report their facts.

So, by the mid-1930s, the definition of objectivity became more diluted and came to refer to reporters' keeping themselves and their opinions out of their stories. In that change, objectivity shifted from being a standard methodology to being a practical posture or orientation of daily reporting.

Even newspaper editors in this modern era define objectivity differently, or at least stress different elements of it as being more important. Several years ago researcher John Boyer studied the attitudes of 50 wire editors—those charged with selecting and editing stories coming in over the newswires—concerning objectivity. A total of 26 different definitions were found among the 50 editors, and the editors fell basically into one of three groups in their definitions. First were the "Balancers," 18 editors who call it objective reporting when both sides are heard and who think objectivity is attainable. Second were the "Skeptics," 17 editors who say objectivity is not attainable but strive instead for balance in the interim while optimizing the reporter's experience. Third were the "Bias Cops," 15 editors who were close to the Balancers, but who felt balance equates more with lack of reporter bias than with telling both sides of the story.[22]

Chapter 2 discussed the various orientations or perspectives journalists bring to their craft. Each of them can influence the objective/subjective nature of a story, but most serious journalists use one or more of the several perspectives to get closer to the truth and, thus, objectivity. For example, when he donned a Detroit Lions football uniform masquerading as a candidate for rookie quarterback in training camp, George Plimpton thought that stance would bring him closer to the reality of what life was actually like for a guy trying to make the Lions' team. He realized it was not a detached approach, insofar as just standing outside and interviewing others in the trenches, but he felt what he gave up in traditional objectivity would be more than compensated by simply getting closer to reality, or the truth of the situation. To him, it was simply reporting from the inside out, rather than the outside in. Others in the journalistic corps disagree heartily with this approach and say objectivity is more achievable by staying detached from the action and people involved.

In recent years, journalists like Jonathan Dube, technology editor of MSNBC.Com, have called for an immersive storytelling similar, in fact, to Plimpton's approach with the Lions. And Dube believes the promise of the new era of multimedia is that, through media convergence (using multiple media tools to tell a story) the journalist can bring the reader or viewer closer to the truth. He cites a story assignment he was given while a student at the Columbia University Graduate School of Journalism. The assignment was to report and present a story for online distribution in New York City. He chose to research a story on teaching subway passengers in Manhattan to be more polite. He used a version of newspaper storytelling and combined it with broadcast techniques to get a converged effect from both media. Wanting to create an entire Web site of ambient storytelling, Dube said he worked to deliver the experience of actually being on a subway platform, with all its sights and sounds, and then to be on the subway car itself. The resulting experience, he believes, was a more complete experience for the reader or viewer.

Reporting the story the same as he would for print, using background research, interviews and first-hand observations, he also brought a tape recorder along and asked a partner to bring a video camera. He was trying for a truly integrated story, an example of what he calls immersive storytelling, putting the reader or viewer in the center of the actual experience. Those following this approach believe it can bring about a greater promise of multimedia: it can get the reader or viewer closer to the truth of the experience.

Dube structured his story into several natural breaks, and put each section on a separate Web page, knowing that research indicates online readers don't like to scroll down copy. He incorporated various photos and sound clips of interviews—as well as natural sounds. He added in useful subway links and information, and he used the icons of the subway cars themselves as a navigational tool. Finally, for the Web site's front page, he combined photos of the subway car doors opening and closing to create an animated picture, and he timed that with the corresponding natural sounds. So the first thing the site user saw was a subway door opening and the first sound they heard was a subway bell ringing. His implied message: "Welcome to my site. Come aboard a New York City subway and let's see what the people are like." The site was a huge hit, and a great example of media convergence to deliver a more complete experience for the consumer.

As discussed in the previous chapter, literary journalism is one of several orientations to the craft of reporting and writing the news. To a strict objectivist, this orientation also poses a challenge to what should be more an arena of report writing. Proponents of literary journalism, such as Tom Wolfe, have been critiqued by traditional journalists for using the techniques of a fiction writer to deliver nonfiction news. In its imperialistic approach of raiding the scene as well as the minds of those persons involved, some editors feel this approach injects too much impressionism into what should be a relatively sterile situation. Wolfe and his followers disagree, however, much the same as George Plimpton might. They argue they are striving for constructing a social autopsy with careful scene-by-scene description, plenty of dialogue, and even a little educated inventing along the way (such as what this individual would probably say in such a situation). In writing like this, literary journalists believe they can approach greater realism by using more of the techniques of narrative storytelling.

Another challenge, at least for some journalists, to traditional objectivity is what could be called the "point-of-view" perspective. Over the years, some journalists have asked whether journalists shouldn't have a point of view in doing a story. Let me try to explain what appears superficially to be a blatant disregard of the objectivist's stance.

Former Secretary of State, Gen. Alexander Haig, once noted, "The press is disembodied; has no life of its own... It lives on the acts of others... It prints what it is given."[23] Reflecting on this observation, a Louisville, Kentucky, newspaper editor said Haig brings up an interesting problem. David Hawpe, managing editor of the *Louisville Courier-Journal,* noted, "I fear Gen. Haig is right... The press cannot live without information, but it has no information of its own. It must rely on others to manufacture the stuff." He added, "We gather great piles of facts, but we seldom assemble them into a point of view."[24]

So why is this a problem? Hawpe continues that relentless factuality creates stories without conclusions and offers muffled reflections of reality where the hard edges of doubt and disagreement are covered and hidden. He and others like him feel this approach is born of a diluted myth of objectivity: the notion that the journalist's job is simply to fetch the truth as a dog would fetch a tossed bone. Hawpe states, "There is one reality out there, and many ways to frame it for readers and viewers. To do that, we must arrive at a point of view about what we find in the world around us...My heresy is I believe in stories with conclusions."[25]

Tapping into this notion of equating factuality with comprehensive reporting, former *Washington Post* Editorial Page Editor Meg Greenfield once wrote an essay with the curious headline, "Misled by the Facts." In it she explained, "We are bombarded by these snippets of facts and lore...we have all these facts, and we think we know more than we actually do."[26] In the process, she asserts, journalists too often confuse knowledge with wisdom, which is more a result of understanding and experience than simple fact gathering.

Hawpe likens fact gathering to stalking deer in the woods and asks is it the journalist's job to simply hunt down the facts, bring them back, and hang them up like a rack of antlers in the journalistic trophy room? If fact hunting is like this, then we ought to ask a few simple questions about the process such as which facts; which stories; reported from which sources, with which questions; using which answers; written how, and packaged in which way? The answer, he says, is found in arriving at some conclusions—at a point of view after the facts are in. This is the process that leads to breaking new ground; relentless factuality is biased toward the status quo.[27]

Arguing with this viewpoint are those journalists like Roger Rosenblatt (see chapter 2) who say conclusions or the larger truth are not even in the purview of daily journalism.

Some journalists, however, argue that Rosenblatt is confusing current practice with correct practice. Just because the nation's news media are obsessed with events rather than issues, does not mean they can't change and embrace issues. Especially so if they find innovative ways of telling those issue stories. Just because poverty may be an untidy issue that seems to be with us all the time doesn't mean a writer like a Rick Bragg, Walt Harrington, or Sebastian Junger can't focus that issue in a story about a homeless person or a Third-World family caught in the midst of the struggle for survival. Why separate the people—the daily journalists—whose job it is to present ongoing reality to readers and viewers, from writers of books or documentaries, or even poets? Why give the latter the corner on truth and confine daily journalists to relentless factuality? Are we as journalists that afraid of trusting our own interpretation; our own understanding of the picture that emerges when one set of facts is linked to the next? If so, are we even qualified to be journalists?

In his book, *The Decision-Making Process in Journalism*, Carl Hausman asserts, "Journalists do miss stories because they don't understand or bother to report the larger set of circumstances that puts events in perspective."[28] He suggests that changing a reporter's perspective can drastically alter the story, just as changing the position of a camera can alter the viewer's perspective on the picture. He cites a situation involving journalist Theodore H. White, a longtime war correspondent in World War II, the Korean War, and Vietnam, who recalled his close-up coverage of warfare in China in 1939:

The Ministry of Information was happy to give me leave. I think my prying had begun to annoy them. They issued me a low-grade military pass to visit the war areas and arranged an airplane ticket to take me to Siam, where I would be on my own to make my way to the war front 250 miles beyond. I was lucky the pass was of such low quality. Had I been granted the VIP pass usually given to famous correspondents and dignitaries, I would have been escorted to the war front and back in style and seen nothing—as happened to me in the Vietnam War, thirty years later, after I had become known and cocooned from reality.[29]

Sometimes objectivity and completeness are simple matters of seeing holes in a reporter's copy and plugging them before they become published holes. Roy Fisher, former dean of the University of Missouri School of Journalism, once described this kind of editing as "defensive editing." He meant anticipating questions readers or viewers might have about the reporting and answering those questions before they get into print. Hausman uses the following example[30] to note how an incomplete thought was translated into a more complete one with the aid of an alert copy editor who challenged the reporter writing the following line of copy:

State College President John J. Smith, who lives in a 15-room mansion overlooking City Park, feels that the park rezoning issue...

The editor found himself asking where Smith gets the money to afford a 15-room mansion in that high-rent neighborhood, given that State College presidents don't make that kind of salary. So he asked the reporter about it, the reporter did some more research, and the following version of that line came about:

State College President John J. Smith, a former senior partner of a major law firm who left corporate law to enter academics five years ago, lives in a 15-room mansion overlooking city Park. He feels that the park rezoning issue...

And now the reader has the question answered and also has a little more of a perspective from which to evaluate Smith's comments about the rezoning issue. Hausman suggests asking the following questions[31] to discern whether a story is objective or not:

- Does the story present the overall perspective? Have the real issues or the cosmetics taken center stage?
- Are there any questions left unanswered or major issues left uncovered?
- Is my perspective objective? As we see in this chapter, objectivity is a thorny issue, but Hausman feels it is safe to assume that if your observations have been controlled in some way, your view is not totally fair.
- Is my intent objective? Be sure your personal feelings do not cloud your treatment of the story.
- Do I have enough material on which to base the story? A story based on one observation or one perspective runs the risk of being unfair and incomplete. In addition, there may be serious omissions of facts, and those can obviously erode the quality and value of a reporter's work.

Writer David T. Z. Mindich wrote an entire book on objectivity in 1998, and made the following observations about the concept:

1. In journalism textbooks, objectivity is alive and well. Of the five most widely used modern textbooks, four specifically tell students to be objective. These texts all discuss objectivity in similar terms, citing the same five components of objective reporting: detachment, nonpartisanship, the inverted-pyramid story structure, naïve empiricism or reliance on facts, and balance.[32]
2. Objectivity as a journalistic strategy dominated the mainstream press for most of the twentieth century.
3. Although many journalists reject the idea of pure objectivity, they still strive for it, define themselves by it, and practice what one media critic has called the "ritual of objectivity," or a series of professional routines designed to shield journalists from blame and legal action.[33]

Assessing the state of objectivity at the turn of the millennium and with the onset of the new online media, Mindich cites CBS News's Dan Rather who drew the following conclusion:

An explosion in news media has again threatened the elite, "objective" journalists. With so many storytellers (each of the thousands of homepages, for example, is a separate news source), and with so many departing from the "information model" of "objective" news, journalists are called on once again to define themselves. It is no surprise that the nature of news and "objectivity" should reemerge as an issue so important to the profession.[34]

For himself, Mindich believes no newscast, CBS or its competitive networks, offer a nightly dose of reality, but instead "mediation between what is out there and what is in here." He concludes, "What we must ask Rather and company is that their filters be better than those of (Bill) O'Reilly and company. What we need Rather to do is explain his filters, to tell us how he interprets reality and why we should buy his interpretation.

To do so would mean abandoning the myth of 'objectivity'...if journalists want to keep the professional ethic they call 'objectivity,' at least they should clearly understand it and be able to argue its merits without claiming 'reality' as a defense." [35]

In so arguing, Mindich feels he is not embracing relativism nor saying the search for truth or balance is impossible. As he puts it, "There is an 'out there' out there...Perhaps the best a reporter can do is to strive to tell the truth, as the reporter sees it, negotiated with his or her editors and readers."[36]

Another journalistic voice questioning the existence of objectivity is Jack Fuller, president and publisher of the *Chicago Tribune*. Fuller has written:

Almost nobody talks about objective reporting any more. What philosophical analysis had not already undermined, radical multiculturalism did. (But) the concept of Objectivity provides as good a starting place as any for the inquiry into the meaning and limitations of the words journalists have used to describe the truth discipline...No one has ever achieved objective journalism, and no one ever could. The bias of the observer always enters the picture, if not coloring the details at least guiding the choice of them. (Bias) is the inevitable consequence of the combination of one's experience and inbred nature. An observer may be able to recognize his biases and attempt to correct for them, but even when this difficult psychological effort occurs, the resulting depiction is still subject, doubly so. The process of correction requires a self-conscious mental intervention that is at odds with the concept of objectivity.[37]

Fuller concludes, somewhat humorously, "Trying to think objectively while recognizing the universality of bias becomes a bit like trying not to think of a purple cow."[38] He says nowhere is objectivity more impossible than when a news organization tries to deal with stories concerning its own personnel or interests. Bad publicity about a media organization's television station or newspaper could hurt the readership or ratings and resulting advertising revenues. That, in turn, could hurt the price of the media company's stock, and that stock is the chief investment vehicle for the company's retirement plan. In spite of this self-interest, the editors at the company newspaper considering the offending report will worry about how the public perceives its handling of an inside story. They know the paper's credibility will be at stake. So tension is inherent in reporting and editing stories about the parent company and its company holdings and, if nothing else, the story will at least receive a great deal more editorial scrutiny than an identical story about another company altogether.

I saw this tension surface a few years ago while helping to edit a newspaper published for a large convention of editors. Even though this was a convention daily published only four times each year during the annual conference, editors understood the importance and sensitivity of stories involving their own newspapers. In this case, the lead story on the first issue of the newspaper concerned the pitched circulation battle between two large dailies in the same host metro area. Editors from both of these dailies were staffing the convention daily, and this one story got more detailed attention from both of them than any other single story during the entire week.

With the current emphasis on storytelling in the journalism profession and with the continual blurring of the lines between soft news and hard news, the concept of objectivity continues to evolve. In a later chapter we will look at some of those newer forms of storytelling, one of which has been called "intimate journalism." A brief description of that story form here will suffice to show its relevance to the continual evolution of how objectivity is defined:

Naturally, the basic rules of news journalism apply to intimate journalism—facts must be correct and context must be fair and accurate. But when it comes to intimate journalism, there's a whole other realm of "facts" that must be collected if we are to achieve our goals—if we are to evoke the worlds of the people we are writing about, describe people and places in enough documentary detail that they seem somehow indisputably real, evoke and describe the inner lives of our subjects, capture a tone in which the reader can, we hope, momentarily forget that this is a story and have the sensation of "felt life" happening before his or her eyes.[39]

This chapter has presented a number of different viewpoints on one of the most often heard terms in journalism: objectivity. It may be the most discussed and least agreed-upon concept in the entire world of the news business. There are good arguments for delivering the news in a variety of ways. One thing, however, seems certain: As the media, its competitive influences, and the desires of its readers and viewers continue to change, so will the way in which news stories are presented. Throughout this evolving process, however, the most serious-minded of the journalists will continue to hold to the fact that their stories are nonfictional essays and not novels, no matter what writing techniques are used to convey those stories to the public.

## NOTES

1. Jaap van Ginneken, *Understanding Global News: A Critical Introduction* (London: Sage, 1998), 65.

2. Ibid.

3. Ibid.

4. Ian O. Lesser et al., *Countering the New Terrorism* (San Francisco: Rand Corporation, 1999), 18ff.

5. Frank Luther Mott, *American Journalism*, (New York: Macmillan, 1962), 232.

6. Ibid., 233.

7. Ibid.

8. Ibid.

9. Ibid., 243.

10. Ibid., 225.

11. Ibid., 524.

12. Ibid., 527.

13. Ibid., 537.

14. Ibid., 529.

15. Louis L. Snyder and Richard B. Morris, eds., *A Treasury of Great Reporting* (New York: Simon and Schuster, 1962), 241.

16. Ibid., 243.

17. Ibid., 245.

18. Ibid., 246–247.

19. Walter Lippmann, *Public Opinion* (New York: Macmillan, 1922), 30–31.

20. Ibid.

21. Philip Meyer, *The New Precision Journalism* (Bloomington: Indiana University Press, 1991), 1–8.

22. John H. Boyer, "How Editors View Objectivity," *Journalism Quarterly* 58 (1): 24.

23. David Hawpe, "Point-of-View Journalism," *Editor & Publisher* (8 September 1984): 40.

24. Ibid.

25. Ibid.

26. Meg Greenfield, "Misled by the Facts," *U.S. News and World Report,* 26 June 1990, 47.

27. Hawpe, "Point-of-View Journalism," 32.

28. Carl Hausman, *The Decision-Making Process in Journalism* (Chicago: Nelson-Hall, 1990), 12.

29. Ibid.

30. Ibid.

31. Ibid.

32. David T. Z. Mindich, *Just the Facts: How "Objectivity" Came to Define American Journalism* (New York: New York University Press, 1998), 8.

33. Ibid., 10.

34. Ibid., 139.

35. Ibid.

36. Ibid.

37. Jack Fuller, *News Values* (Chicago: University of Chicago Press, 1996), 14.

38. Ibid.

39. Walt Harrington, *Intimate Journalism: The Art and Craft of Reporting Everyday Life* (Thousand Oaks, Calif.: Sage, 1997), xx–xxi.

# Chapter 4

# Scientific Journalism: What It Is and What It Isn't

If one were to put reporting perspectives on a scale from psychological detachment to psychological involvement, one end of the scale would be anchored by the concept of scientific journalism, and the other would be anchored by the concept of intimate journalism. Chapter 2 looked briefly at scientific journalism, but it's time to look deeper into this approach to evaluate its advantages and disadvantages for journalists and the stories they produce.

The basis of scientific journalism—or precision journalism as it later came to be known—is that reporters get the story wrong too often either for factual or subjective reasons. Subjective reasons might include misplaced story emphasis, distorted mood, imbalance, and so on. Some of these errors can be relatively minor, but others can affect the entire meaning or truth of a story.

Writing early in the twentieth century, journalist/philosopher Walter Lippmann suggested that an antidote to the kind of sensationalistic yellow journalism the country had just experienced was for journalists to take more of a scientific approach to journalism. By that, he and others meant journalists should think more like scientists when pursuing facts and follow parts of the scientific method in their reporting. In so doing, they could come closer to being objective and letting the facts speak for themselves, apart from journalistic coloration. Decades later, journalistic scholar William Rivers noted in his study of fact-finding that natural scientists are not too dismayed when they discover the fact they once respected can no longer be considered valid. In many cases, replacing one fact or theory with another is a cause for rejoicing in the scientific community. New facts and resulting theories that are trustworthy rely on a foundation that can be trusted, so researchers must work on solid, tested ground. To be sure, there is always the human element in scientific research, however. No researcher who has built a reputation on developing a usable theory wants to see his or her work depicted as faulty or incomplete by another researcher with a study that disproves or diminishes his. Still, scientists know that theories only become laws when proven over and over again in subsequent studies.

Rivers uses an analysis suggested by Henri Poincare to illustrate the depth and range of the knowledge that a scientist might bring to a problem:

Suppose we have before us any machine; the initial wheel work and the final wheel work alone are visible, but the transmission, the intermediary other, is hidden in the interior and escapes our view; we do know whether the communication is made by gearing or by belts, by connecting rods or by other contrivances. Do we say that it is impossible for us to understand this machine because we are not permitted to take it to pieces? You know well that we do not, And that the principle of conservation of energy suffices to determine for us the most interesting point. We easily ascertain that the final wheel turns ten times less quickly than the initial wheel, since these two wheels are visible; we are able thence to conclude that a couple applied to the one will be balanced by a couple ten times greater applied to the other. For that there is no need to penetrate the mechanism of this equilibrium and to know how the forces compensate each other in the interior of the machine.[1]

On a much higher level, Rivers notes this kind of reasoning about hidden mechanisms led to the theory of gravity, the theory of organic evolution, and the theory of relativity. The scientific method then emphasizes the pursuit of facts and knowledge through observation—systematic observation. As researcher Frederick Williams points out, "Whatever is said about behavior is reasoned from systematic observation and is tested and retested by observation. In other words, the so-called scientific approach attempts to anchor knowledge in terms of the physical reality it purports to explain."[2]

In journalistic reporting, the scientific approach leads a reporter to such systematic observation, using inductive and deductive reasoning to be explained shortly. The approach of intimate journalism would lead one to anecdotal reporting and to looking inside Rivers's machine to show the parts in action. This latter approach is more impressionistic, in that different journalists might describe differently the same phenomenon because of the way the observed person strikes them. On the other hand, in using systematic observation as the cornerstone of his or her approach, the scientific journalist would apply a rigorous procedure to guide him or her in pursuing the truth. Journalists can find an outline of these procedures in one of their own academic journals: *Journalism and Mass Communication Quarterly*. For example, a typical *J&MC Quarterly* article is divided as follows:

- An introductory discussion of the issue to be studied and why that issue is important.
- A review of all relevant literature that features the results of previous studies conducted about this issue.
- A statement of the hypotheses to be tested in the current study, how they were developed and why they are important.
- A detailed statement of the methodology employed in collecting, observing, and analyzing the data to test the hypotheses. Usually this methodology is the most important part of the whole process, and results can stand or fall on the validity and reliability of this methodology.
- A detailed statement of findings once the collected data has been analyzed.
- A more generalized discussion of the results and conclusions drawn and what they might imply for the issue under observation.

A couple concepts that prove vitally important to the scientist are validity and reliability. Essentially, validity of measurement is the extent to which the researcher measures what he or she purports to be measuring. Reliability addresses the issue of whether, using the same measuring instrument, these results would surface again and again in future tests.[3] A reliable test is one that has no internal or external contaminating factors, if such a test can actually exist. Breaking these two concepts down, one could use the analogy of a set of bathroom scales. If scales were used to measure your weight instead of some other characteristic such as total fitness, then they are a valid instrument, albeit limited in their use. That assumes they are calibrated correctly, of course. You can assume from this validity that these same scales are also a reliable instrument. They measure accurately now and, unless something happens to them, they will measure accurately tomorrow. Thus, validity implies reliability, although reliability does not necessarily imply validity. You could have a reliable set of scales that are calibrated incorrectly and that therefore are not valid. If the scales weigh two pounds light, for instance, everyone who gets on them will have a weight showing that is two pounds lighter than reality. Thus the scales will be consistent, but consistently wrong.

Validity and reliability are important twin concepts when designing a measuring instrument such as a survey or field experiment. There are definite rules, for example, in governing the creation of a random sample. If these rules are broken, the sample is not truly random and the measuring instrument is internally flawed or invalid. Thus the results will be off.

Earlier I mentioned the concepts of inductive and deductive reasoning. To understand the scientific approach to fact-finding, one should know something about these. Research literature from the social and behavioral sciences is used to emphasize the logic of deductive reasoning, in which a hypothesis is stated or implied in the assumptions guiding the project. The researcher proceeds, then, from the general to the particular. From a set of assumptions, the researcher deduces the hypothesis—for instance, the more a child watches violence on television, the more prone he or she will be to act out violence in real life.

This deductive approach stands in contrast to inductive reasoning in which the researcher moves inferentially from the particulars to a more general conclusion. Induction is used continuously, both in problem definition and in interpreting the results. For example, a researcher might observe a case in which a person's tension leads to avoidance of certain communications and, as a result, infer a general relationship between tension and avoidance. Generalizing from measured results is also an inductive process, such as when behavior among a sample of individuals is generalized to a larger population.

In reality, scientists use both induction and deduction, either at the same time or alternatively. One could deduce, for example, that given a set of assumptions about the effects of a certain drug, aggressive behavior might result. However, consideration of this reasoning might lead to the realization, arrived at inductively, that such a drug might have other consequences as well. The researcher may have observations indicating that a certain drug might produce dependency on it by the patient. Then, generalizing from this observation (an inductive process), the investigator may use a new deductive methodology to prove that association.

One source of conflict between the scientist and the journalist is how the individual case or individual observation is perceived, and the kind of impact it is allowed to have on the final conclusion. To a researcher, a case is a single unit of observation to be assimilated into many other cases, from which some statistical trend may arise. It is that statistically significant trend that is important to the researcher and it is that that he or she writes about. To the journalist, on the other hand, statistics need to be fleshed out in human terms. The editor or producer believes the reader or viewer will change channels if they are presented with sterile, statistical information, devoid of personality or a human face. What they strive for is to show how the larger problem plays out in individual persons. Therefore, most medical stories that appear in newspapers or on TV began, at least, with an individual focus or anecdotal lead. This single anecdote is fleshed out, developed, detailed, and amplified throughout several stages before the story may swing into the segment that discusses the overall trend. Some stories, in fact, make short shrift of the statistical picture and choose instead to stay focused on the individual case. This is done in the narrative storytelling structure in which the story never deviates from the development of the individual case.

This use of anecdotal evidence is something most researchers find inappropriate in proving anything. After all, to them, a single case is just that. You cannot generalize from it with any degree of statistical specificity. To the journalist, on the other hand, the focus often is the single case. The conclusion, either direct or indirect, is that this person's plight is typical of many other individuals with the same problem. Journalists have always liked to use anecdotal evidence. It is the stuff of the human interest story and, more now than ever, is also a key substance of news stories of all kinds. Putting societal problems into human terms is a great way to evoke emotional response and—hopefully—bring concerted action to bear on the problem. These stories are much more moving than the statistical treatises that the research journals publish, although the evidence they present for their conclusions is anecdotal and may not be truly representative of the wider population afflicted with a problem. Nevertheless, because these stories grab the attention of readers and viewers, they also grab the attention of politicians who will often shift their legislative agendas to move these topics to the forefront for action. This can be good or bad, depending on how accurate the representations presented in the anecdotes actually are.

Popularizing scientific journalism in the 1960s was Philip Meyer, professor of journalism at the University of North Carolina. Meyer argued for what he called "precision journalism," as a means of going beneath the surface of news events and as added insurance for reporter accuracy. As desktop computer development gained speed in the 1970s and 1980s, the possibilities for scientific journalism increased. Now journalistic researchers had in their grasp the means to analyze data and even apply statistical tests to it themselves. The main application for journalists has been in the area of computer-assisted reporting, or simply using the vast amounts of information available on the internet to deepen and round out their reporting. More intrepid journalists set up their own database management systems and analyze databases kept by public agencies, looking for patterns and hidden meanings behind the rhetoric of public officials.

Writing in his *New Precision Journalism* in 1991, Meyer said of the concept:

Knowing what to do with data is the essence of the new precision journalism. The problem may be thought of as having two phases: the input phase, where data are collected and analyzed, and the output phase, where the data are prepared for entry into the reader's mind...Modern scientific method provides for aggressive reality testing. Journalists are interested in testing reality, too. The main difference—beyond the obvious one that journalists are in more of a hurry—is that journalists are more passive about it. Instead of testing reality directly with their own observations, deductions and experiments, they are normally content to do their cross-checking by consulting different authorities with different viewpoints and different interests.[4]

Meyer notes that reporters and editors already understand some of the traits of the scientific method and employ it unconsciously in their own pursuit of facts. Among these traits are:

- Skepticism. Neither journalists nor scientists are content to rest with what popular opinion or authority claims is true. Additionally, the idea of truth is always tentative, and always has room for revision and improvement.

- Openness. This is an idea that can be equated with replication in the scientific world. An investigative journalist is usually open with the public about his search for truth and leaves a visible trail of how he got his information so others could—if they wanted—search out the same facts.

- An instinct for operationalization. The process of finding the observable and testable phenomenon is called operationalization. Both scientists and investigative reporters depend on it and look for feasible and generalizable subjects to test, interview, observe, or probe.

- Parsimony. "Given a choice between rival theories, we generally prefer the simpler one," Meyer writes.[5] "The best theory explains the most with the least." Most journalists seem to believe this idea, as do scientists.

Nevertheless, journalists take pride in their independence, autonomy, and creativity in the ways they chase facts. And they use all of these—often in unorthodox ways—to ferret out the truth. In contrast to the scientist who painstakingly follows an elaborate and time-tested scientific method in pursuing the answer to a single question, the journalist pursues a number of leads at once. In so doing, she chases a number of phenomena posing as fact and must treat them all as equally valid until verification proves them to be truth, lie, or rumor. And the verification the normal reporter seeks is often something less than a scientist would accept as proof. As Meyer says, reporters usually substitute multiple sources—something they often call "triangulation"—for the scientific method of systematic observation and analysis. Additionally, reporters often find it necessary to take shortcuts to obtaining facts, especially on deadline. Case in point: a reporter has only 15 minutes to deadline and is having trouble obtaining the medical status of a patient who was recently hit by a car. So he calls the hospital nursing station and announces himself as the victim's brother who desperately wants to know his brother's condition. So if one avenue to the facts is blocked, the resourceful journalist will take another route, one often overlooked by the novice traveler. Therefore, the rigidity of the scientific method might often pose problems for the creative-minded journalists.

Having said this, however, it would be incorrect to think journalists don't follow a pattern—if not a system—in pursuing many facts. More often than not, it is a general set of guidelines that leads them, including the following:

- Seeking out credible sources.
- Finding multiple sources on key stories and/or on key points within stories.
- Pursuing the so-called paper trail of evidence before interviewing sources who are the actual targets of the story. The feeling is this makes it easier to spot when a source is lying or misleading the reporter.

- Attempting to remain detached and objective from the story as much as possible, although a growing number of reporters wonder if this really gets the journalist closer to the truth of a situation or if it may act as a roadblock. More will be said about this in a later chapter.
- Attempting to be fair and balanced in covering all relevant sides to the story.
- Attempting to be accurate with the information provided or ferreted out.
- Trying to present the information in an appropriate story structure, answering all the questions the readers might have about the event, person, or issue.

In the end, however, journalists are very human and many are creatures of habit and routines. Often the reporter's routine is the problem, however, especially if it leads to expedient reporting at the cost of comprehensive reporting. A study in *Journalism and Mass Communication Quarterly*,[6] for instance, found the following from a sample of metro dailies:

- Reporters do much of the background information retrieval that informs their work, but their focus is very narrow and conventional when they search. In large measure, they look only at the own newspaper's electronic backfiles as they prepare their breaking news stories.
- Reporters still turn to the same official sources as were apparent in more classic newsmaking studies. Even though they use more of these officials in each story, the range of sources has not expanded.
- Reporters are not using external databases enough to help them break out of the official source syndrome. In other words, they are still relying on the same sources as always—either by new interview or old backfile—instead of looking beyond their own library to retrieve other sources of information. With increased use of the Internet, however, this pattern may change some.

The researchers note another interesting aspect in concluding this study:

The conventions of objectivity appear to be firmly in place. The evidence from this study indicates that journalists are reluctant to openly question statements by interviewees. They may include another source's skepticism about an interviewee's assertions, but the journalists themselves rarely include their own fact statements or interpretations in their breaking news stories. This reluctance persists despite the fact that reporters and editors may have, through the use of electronic information retrieval systems, access to far more information about the topic or issue than the interviewee.[7]

The best of both worlds might be to bring together the perspectives of a journalist with elements of the scientific method, when appropriate. The news will always have to have a human face if it is to appeal at all to readers or viewers. The individual anecdote is still the best way of showing readers what the larger issue is all about and how it impacts everyday people. So doing trend stories that are told in people-oriented fashion seems a good way to go. Reporters can incorporate elements of the scientific process into their everyday routines and beats by paying attention to what Keir, McCombs, and Shaw call "social indicators." They point out there are many potential hypotheses journalists can explore in every town, and they call for reporters to exercise strategic planning in organizing comprehensive coverage that is built upon these indicators.[8]

Essentially a social indicator is an index of a particular trend. It may be the monthly report from the city's building inspector that lists the number of new housing permits sought and granted for that 30-day period. In comparing that indicator with the one from the previous month or the same month a year ago, reporters might spot a trend up or down in new construction. Another social indicator might be a monthly report issued by the local Social Services Department showing the number of elderly persons in the community who used the Senior Citizens Center for that period of time. These and myriad other reports can track physical, social, and economic trends in a community over time. Many of them are issued in numerical form and are easily analyzed by various computer statistical programs that check for significance of the trend analyzed.

Although the idea of a hypothesis might seem stilted and even intimidate a daily newspaper reporter, the fact is that journalists use hypotheses all the time in their reporting work. In fact it is usually such a hunch that gets them focused on a particular question or issue to research in the first place as a possible story idea. The old idea of a nose for news simply refers to a reporter who spots what he or she believes to be a hypothesis worth testing through normal reporting methodology. Sometimes called a "slant" or "angle" to a story, or even a focus, it is what keeps the reporter and the story on track. It offers clues to the reporter about who should be interviewed, what should be observed, and which documents to search for and analyze. In short, daily journalism is really a form of hypothesis testing on deadline. The advantage a reporter has over a social scientist is that his or her news beat offers entrée every day into a world of data and information that are essentially individual social indicators. When pieced together in a form of a mosaic—which is what reporters do when they write their stories—a larger and more understandable picture emerges of what is really going on, outside the event itself.

For example, Keir, McCombs, and Shaw point out that the health status of a community is well documented by public health departments operating at nearly every level of government, local, state, and national. The data available to reporters runs the gamut from the incidence of dozens of diseases that are reported by doctors and hospitals, to the amount of money spent on various kinds of treatments from public funds. These indicators form the basis for stories dealing with the physical health of the town's residents and also add to the ongoing national debate on the needs and status of health care.[9]

The researchers describe "The Nine Nations of North America," a reporting plan created by *Washington Post* editor Joel Garreau, as a classic example of good strategic planning.[10] Garreau's aim in developing the plan was to assist his reporters in seeing and understanding the trends and patterns that exist just below the surface in the news. The perspective is founded upon a rich view of North American regionalism. Garreau delineates nine regions in all that stretch beyond the boundaries of the United States to encompassing part of northern Mexico, the Caribbean Basin, and Canada. Garreau explains:

Each has a peculiar economy; each commands a certain emotional allegiance from its citizens. These nations look different, feel different, and sound different from each other, and few of their boundaries match the political lines drawn on current maps. Some are clearly divided topographically by mountains, deserts, and rivers. Others are separated by architecture, music, language, and ways of making a living. Each nation has its own list of desires...Most important each nation has a distinct prism through which it views the world.[11]

Reporting through this grid offers a strategic view that, even if only applied in a single region, offers endless tactical variations. For example, "There are Texans who are content that their state itself is seven distinct 'nations.' Other observers advocate splitting California into two states because of strong regional differences that undergird debate on a wide variety of public issues."[12] This regionalizing—or looking for regional patterns—can be applied in any geographical area, large or small, and can be used to help explain the difference existing among people on a single issue or several issues. There are bound to be a lot of social indicators kept by various government agencies at all levels that help to detail these regional differences among people.

Incorporating the use of social indicators into their daily reporting schedule can add depth and greater insight into a reporter's stories over time. If you were to compare a normal daily reporter to a lighthouse beam scanning the ocean's horizon, you would find that reporter latching onto any event, issue, or person that protrudes above the surface of the water and that is visible to the naked eye. Using social indicators, however, could be analogous to employing sonar beams in the search. With these, reporters can not only skim the surface but also look deep beneath the water to see what foundations or elements are causing the protrusion—and possibly even causing that protrusion to shift places from time to time.

Part of the debate about incorporating statistical indices and the scientific method into the work of a daily reporter is that many journalists are skeptical of statistics—or at least the way they are used by news sources. Nowhere is the attempt at manipulation of the media more prevalent than in the spin that various sources might put on the same set of statistics. Even journalists themselves do it. When I began my career in journalism, for example, my first job was as news editor of a twice-a-week newspaper that loved to boost the community every chance it got. One of the standing stories we did every month was the building inspector's report. This town was in a high-growth spiral, and the newspaper publisher wanted to do his part in helping the trend continue. Part of this involved keeping a positive emphasis on that growth and instilling in people's minds that things are going great in the area construction industry. So I was quickly instructed to find a positive message in the monthly building inspector's report, especially in the stats showing the number of new housing and business permits approved. "There are a number of ways you can draw positive conclusions, even if the report is showing fewer housing starts," my publisher would say. None of those ways involved lying, but they did involve emphasizing different things in searching for positive conclusions. So if the number of overall housing starts was done for the period, I'd look for, say, the number of permits granted for upper-range, more expensive homes. If that segment of the housing permits showed growth from the previous month, I'd focus on it. Or perhaps there would be growth in the more affordable homes. Hence another approach to the story, but one also with a positive spin.

Another reason journalists are skeptical about developing statistical portraits is that, as a rule, journalists are intimidated by math and numbers. It's only natural, because most journalists are more verbal than quantitative in their personal orientations. They prefer words and creating verbal expressions over numbers and numerical calculations. Occasionally you find journalists who excel on both the verbal and quantitative scales, but not very often. For two years I taught statistics to graduate journalism students, and I can attest to the fact that verbally-oriented students are not at ease around numbers, nor are they enchanted by them.

This brings up another rift between those scientists or researchers who use statistical significance as the main basis of their documenting truth, and journalists who use something less empirical for that foundation, but something that seems painfully clear to them. To a journalist, statistics don't tell the whole story and can, in fact, be misleading. Some phenomena also are simply beyond the range of empirical testing (take documenting causal effects of television and violence among viewers, for example). Instead, if a reporter can find an individual or a group of individuals who resemble a larger population caught up in a particular problem or issue, they will focus on those individuals and tell their story anecdotally and in narrative fashion. To these journalists, this is real-life documentation, regardless of whether a scientist might chide them for not following the scientific method in devising that random sample or in observing it or analyzing the results.

Many reporters try to satisfy the rigors of both the well-written story and the need for harder documentation by writing in a structure that has come to be known as the *Wall Street Journal* Format or one of its variations.

In this format, the reporter identifies whom he or she feels is a typical person caught up in the dilemma being reported on and written about. The story begins with a relevant anecdote—often an extended one—that sets the focus for the piece in individual, human terms. Then, through the use of a bridge or nut graph, the writer swings from that anecdote to the larger issue featured in the story. That issue may then be written in a more traditional inverted-pyramid format, interspersing references to the individual case discussed in the opening anecdote. The ending of the piece may loop back to that individual again and close out with an individual focus. Actually, this is the form many stories are told in these days.

In fact, the mandates normally ascribed to responsible journalism today demand that the individual journalist use all of these techniques and approaches in constructing his or her story. The marketplace demands that the story be entertaining and, even were that not the case, most good journalists would want to engage their readers with a well-written story. And the credibility of the reporter and the story demand that accuracy be paramount, and that the reporter use the hardest documentation he or she can find for the points asserted in that story. Some of that documentation may be individual case studies of people caught up in an issue or problem, but part of it should also be based upon empirical evidence of the kind systematic observation provides.

## NOTES

1. William Rivers, *Finding Facts: Interviewing, Observing, Using Reference Sources* (Englewood Cliffs, N.J.: Prentice-Hall, 1975), 10.

2. Frederick Williams, *Reasoning with Statistics* (New York: Holt, Rinehart and Winston, 1968), 3.

3. Frederick Williams as quoted in Jim Willis, *Reporting on Risks* (Westport, Conn.: Praeger, 1997), 43–44.

4. Philip Meyer, *The New Precision Journalism* (Bloomington: Indiana University Press, 1991), 8.

5. Ibid., 13.

6. Kathleen A. Hansen et al., "Local Breaking News: Sources, Technology, and News Routines," *Journalism and Mass Communication Quarterly*, 71, no. 3 (1994): 566–569.

7. Ibid.

8. Gerry Keir, Maxwell McCombs, and Donald Shaw, *Advanced Reporting: Beyond News Events* (Prospect Heights, Ill.: Waveland Press, 1991), 231ff.

9. Ibid.

10. Ibid.

11. Ibid.

12. Ibid.

# Chapter 5

# The Human Journalist: Getting Up Close and Personal

A major portion of this book has focused on the objectivist/subjectivist debate in journalism circles. How close should journalists get to the action, issues, and people they write about? Is distancing yourself from an event a good thing or a bad thing? Shouldn't we retain the traditional line between news and feature stories and also retain the way in which we write those stories? Or have the rules all changed? Is there any need to separate the two forms of storytelling out from each other? Certainly the concept of scientific journalism or precision journalism would run counter to a more anecdotal or individualistic-oriented approach, but so would the traditional reporting perspectives, such as the Joe Friday Perspective discussed in chapter 2.

In recent years journalists have focused much attention on storytelling as a way of presenting a nonfiction story creatively. Editors see in this approach a way of winning readers back to a newspaper they may have come to see as too stuffy, arrogant, or sterile, detached, and uncaring about the community problems written about in their news columns. The term "intimate journalism" was coined by former *Washington Post* magazine reporter Walt Harrington, now a professor of journalism at the University of Illinois.[1] Harrington has written important profiles of George Bush, Jesse Jackson, Jerry Falwell, Lynda Bird Johnson Robb, and Carl Bernstein, in addition to many profiles of ordinary people not normally in the limelight. He is the author of *Crossings: A White Man's Journey into Black America*, and *American Profiles: Somebodies and Nobodies Who Matter*, and *At the Heart of It: Ordinary People, Extraordinary Lives*. Harrington likens the reporter to a person who has the job of "remembering for the tribe."[2] He believes we remember many things very well (that is, the state of the Dow Jones average, the death of a celebrity, a coup in Argentina.) But he feels too many important memories slip through the fingers of the journalists and, therefore, from the collective consciousness of the tribe for which that journalist writes. Among these kinds of memories are the following:[3]

- The feeling a child gets when she takes the power of the Holy Spirit into her heart at first communion.
- The feeling an old farmer has when he latches his barn door for the last time on the night before his homestead is sold.
- The feeling a teacher gets when a bad student becomes a good one.
- The feeling a mother has when her daughter pitches the winning game in the Little League championship.
- The feeling a father has when he must bury his son.

Harrington explains:

On the banks of the stream that is our civilization, these emotions are life. As sportswriter and novelist Dan Jenkins puts it, "Life its ownself." But to most journalists honored with the job of remembering the stories of the tribe, these momentous events of everyday life are virtually invisible. To most American journalists, such events are akin to the dark and unknown matter believed to make up 90 percent of the universe. We keep reporting the movement of the planets when the big news is the unseen matter in which they spin. At best, most journalists are oblivious to reporting the incredible human beauty and subtlety that surround them. At worst, they militantly oppose reporting and what they are untrained to discern and describe. But either way, readers are being denied a look at much of the world they inhabit. In the language of the craft, we're missing the story."[4]

To Harrington and others like him, this is where intimate journalism enters the picture. "It was years before I thought of 'intimate journalism' as a sub-genre of literary journalism, which may or may not attempt to evoke the subjective realities of subjects, either famous or obscure, but which inevitably uses reporting and writing techniques aimed at giving nonfiction a more storylike quality...The simple goal of intimate journalism should be to describe and evoke how people live and what they value," Harrington says. "...everything ordinary and everything extraordinary in our lives."[5]

Many of the techniques of this people-focused storytelling should sound familiar because they were ones championed by other literary journalists like Tom Wolfe in the 1960s and 1970s. The techniques include:[6]

- Thinking, reporting and writing in scenes.
- Capturing a narrator's voice and/or writing the story from the point of view of one or several subjects.

- Gathering telling details from the subjects' lives; details that evoke the tone of that life.
- Gathering real-life dialogue, which creates the sense of life happening before readers' eyes.
- Gathering interior monologue—what the subjects are thinking, feeling, imagining, dreaming, or worrying about.
- Reporting to establish a time line that allows us to develop a narrative story with a beginning, middle, and end.
- Immersing ourselves temporarily in the lives of our subjects so they become relaxed in our presence.
- Gathering physical details of places and people.
- Always being aware that no matter how artful our stories may be...they are primarily meant to enlighten, caution, criticize or inspire, always resonate, in the lives of readers.
- Remembering the glue that holds all of this together is the fact that, as Tom Wolfe once said, "All of this is true, right down to the breed of the dog and the brand of the beer."

It is reporting and writing that bring to bear all of the journalist's senses on the story he or she is presenting. It is the kind of story that emerges when former *New York Times* reporter Rick Bragg writes one of his patented profiles of ordinary people like professional down-and-outer Gangaram Mahes of New York City in the story, "A Thief Dines out, Hoping Later to Eat in."

Every now and then, Gangaram Mahes slips on his best donated clothes and lives the high life. He strolls to a nice restaurant, sips a fine aperitif, savors a $50 meal and finishes with hot black coffee. The waiters call him sir, but Mr. Mahes could not dig a dollar from his pocket for a bus ride to heaven.

He is a thief who never runs, a criminal who picks his teeth as the police close in. To be arrested, to go home to a cell at Rikers Island, is his plan when he unfolds his napkin.

Homeless off and on for several years, he steals dinner from the restaurants because he wants the courts to return him to a place in New York where he is guaranteed three meals a day and a clean bed. In a prison system filled with repeat offenders, the 36-year-old Mr. Mahes is a serial diner.[7]

Or it is the kind of story former *Los Angeles Times* reporter Barry Bearak wrote about a young woman in west Texas whose life was changed by meeting the Deity:

LUBBOCK, Tex.—From the mists above and a hunger within, Theresa Werner thought she saw God. He seemed so much like the paintings.

His hair was white and his eyes were fire. The rumble of his voice was at once a comfort and a fright.

"Convert your ways, for time shall erase all men's memories," he said.

And that was just the once. Other days it was the Virgin Mary who spoke to her. Our Lady lamented the sinners and warned of chastisements. In her diary, Theresa wrote: Can this really be happening? I am so unsure.[8]

Some journalists might say this kind of approach is fine for a feature story, but not for a hard news story. But that assumes that everyone defines a hard news story in the same way. The first of these two leads sat on a story that was essentially about homelessness in New York City, a very real and significant problem to that city, its residents, and visitors.

The second lead topped a story about one of the most divisive issues to hit west Texas Catholics in quite some time and one that occasioned an official Papal task force visit to the area to determine whether there had in fact been a visit by the Virgin Mary. If a hard news story is defined as an issue-oriented story as well as an event-oriented story, then these two examples qualify. And if hard news doesn't encompass issues as well as singular events, one might legitimately wonder why not.

For his "Visions of Holiness in Lubbock," Bearak (who moved on to the *New York Times*) won the National Journalism Writing Award, presented by Nixon Newspapers and the School of Journalism at Ball State University. In his acceptance speech to students and faculty at Ball State, Bearak said he is always looking for the unusual angle or viewpoint to take into a story, whether it is a news story or a feature story. He noted that the Lubbock story could have been told more traditionally, from the standpoint of the clergy and the Catholic Church officials who were on the scene investigating Theresa Werner's assertions. In fact, he said, that is how many newspapers did report it. But it was also a very boring way of telling the story, albeit a safe way, and also a very predictable way. Want to know why readers are leaving newspapers? This is one of them.

Instead, Bearak advised students to seek the unique viewpoints to stories. For example, he said he once covered a story about a controversy between commercial fishermen and sport fishermen in Canadian waters over fishing for cod. As he began to report that story, Bearak said he realized he could have told the story from the viewpoint of the commercial fishermen or from the sport fishermen. Or, he winked, he could have told it from the viewpoint of the codfish, which probably would have been the most entertaining and offbeat. Although Bearak was having a little fun with his audience to make his point, I do remember reading a well-written history (albeit a historical novel) of General Robert E. Lee of Civil War fame, a book called *Traveler*, that was told through the eyes of General Lee's famed white horse on whose back he led the Confederacy in fighting that bloody war. And in reading it, my thoughts kept returning to Bearak and his advice to journalists to seek out the unusual viewpoint for the story.

Not convinced about the legitimacy of focusing hard news stories first on the people impacted by these events or issues? Take a look at the opening paragraphs of a breaking news story about a significant event: the ten-year anniversary of the fall of the Berlin Wall on November 9, 1999:

To the "Ossis" it was a monster standing menacingly between them and freedom. To the "Wessis" it was a constant reminder that a third of their homeland had been abducted, possibly forever.

Both East and West Germans wanted the Berlin Wall to fall. Both were equally shocked as the rest of the world when it did, exactly 10 years ago Tuesday.

Like a singer who labors for years in obscurity and then lands the break making her an overnight success, the menace of the Berlin Wall vanished November 9, 1989, in the blink of an eye that took almost three decades to shut.

During those 28 years the Wall created a lot of heroes among the Easterners who refused to give up on seeking freedom.

There were the five East Germans who took a brown Opel P4 and turned it into a bulletproof car by welding armor plating to its interior and pouring concrete into the side panels. They squeezed in and careened it through the East Berlin checkpoint amid a hail of police gunfire on November 14, 1961.

There was the East German university student who was the first to successfully fly a 6-foot, self-built escape aircraft to freedom on August 4, 1984. The flight plan consisted of a terror-filled 100-meter ride at low altitude over the Wall.

Three years later, there was the brave mother who covered her 4-year-old son in a shopping bag, put it on a shopping cart and strolled calmly onto a subway in East Berlin to use a day pass to buy household goods in West Berlin. She had heard that border guards rarely checked the contents of bags on a shopping day, although sometimes they could surprise you. On this day, May 4, 1987, they didn't and mother and son found their freedom.

These were some of the lucky ones. One thousand East Germans died from 1949 to 1989 trying to flee the East, while 764 of those died since the Wall went up in August of 1961.

These stories were all part of the legacy that this horde of spirited Germans commemorated outside on the new government plaza here Tuesday night in damp 40-degree weather. Despite mixed feelings of some countrymen, these Berliners were here to say they're glad the Wall is now gone.[9]

This example raises an important aspect of the kind of people-oriented or intimate journalism that Harrington, Bragg, Bearak, Wolfe, and countless other journalists now prefer. It is not an easy kind of journalism to do because it requires intense research and demands a creative writing style that both engages the reader and stays true to the facts and larger truth of the story. You don't make up the anecdotes for a nonfiction story, although you may well create the analogies, similes, or metaphors you use. You don't make up the dialogue; in fact, you don't invent anything at all except the way in which you tell the story.

For the journalist who wants to suspend the blur of events for a moment to focus in on one of the marchers who would be representative of many around him, the way of telling the story involves focusing on individuals or small, identifiable groups. Those are the ones readers and viewers can identify with and, even though there is no systematic and time-tested formula at work for randomly selecting these individuals, the journalist is given some credit for picking out those who seem representative—or even unique—to him or her. These become individual case studies, much as the anthropologist might select them. Spending time with them, engaging in dialogue and deep conversations, observing and taking copious notes, talking with friends of the subject—and even enemies if there are any—ultimately can yield a comprehensive and truthful account of those individuals and the larger problem within which they are trapped. Knowing how they react—seeing them in action—gives the reader or viewer an insightful view of what life is like for the others caught in the similar problem.

One such writing coach who counsels journalists to put real, identifiable people in their news stories is Donald Fry, formerly of the Poynter Institute for Media Studies and now a writing coach for a number of news organizations. In discussing this with several hundred journalists in a Portland, Oregon, National Writer's Workshop, Fry outlined the following[10]—among other—principles of writing about people:

- Remember that news is about people and not about data.
- Television uses talking heads; newspapers use talking names. Avoid both.
- Real people in stories come from real people in reporting becoming real people in the notebook.
- Officials and high-ranking people can be real people, but they try their best not to, and we aid and abet that effort.
- Let the reader see and hear people in the story in action, on site.
- Select the characters in a story rigorously.
- People don't speak quotes. Quote people in real speech.
- Describe gestures and actions more than things.
- Select details that reveal character, and develop that character with little touches.
- Reactions from other people characterize powerfully.
- Don't read minds, but don't hesitate to convey thought and emotion if you have the evidence.
- All stories have a teller, and the storyteller is also a character with a unique voice. Give a credible and appropriate voice to your story.

This is important to the theme of this book because this writing approach will probably wind up revealing more than thought patterns of the individuals. At its best it will reveal the intensity with which the individual is thinking and feeling. It presupposes that most readers and viewers are more interested in what a person's gut feeling is than what his or her intellect is telling him or her to think or say. And it presupposes that showing an individual in action—reacting to various stimuli—is a great way of showing how he or she is feeling and how deep the intensity of that feeling really is. In many ways, it is the polar opposite approach of the scientific journalist who is more concerned about what a random sample of the group says about the individuals than the other way around. Both approaches have their place in journalism today but, in most cases, this more intimate approach is the one readers would rather tune in.

Fry offers the following example of some of these principles. It is a story about the forgotten earthquake that struck California's bay area in the wake of the more severe San Francisco quake. It is a story that injects real people, right from the start, to the action and then moves to the larger story through a nut graph that ends this passage:

Patty Hermann is leading the way through her house. The kitchen is bad—cracked walls, broken dishes. The dining room is bad, too—more cracks, plaster everywhere. Then comes the living room, the room that two days after the earthquake, Hermann won't go in.

In this room, there is no longer an outside wall. There is only a wide hole where the wall was, and a sagging, unsupported roof. There is also a TV set, still plugged in, still tuned to the channel showing the World Series, but Patty Hermann is too afraid to retrieve it.

"We are working up our nerve," Mark Hermann, Patty's husband, says.

"Sickening, isn't it?" says Patty. "It was," she adds, "a spectacular house."

It was, indeed, and it is no more. Instead, it is unsalvageable. It is the most severely damaged structure in Los Gatos, and, in its own way, it illustrates how there wasn't one earthquake in northern California Tuesday, but two.[11]

Whereas the traditional journalist might well start this story with summary information from the last paragraph—that there were two earthquakes in the bay area and not just one—this writer chose to start with a lead that people could identify with and that still gets the larger point across.

And there is the following example of the top of a story about a city of 65,000 people that was in the path of the monstrous F-5 twister in central Oklahoma the evening of May 3, 1999. The story is told from the viewpoint of a few hundred of the city's residents attending a ceremony at the local high school:

Two signal events provided the drama in Midwest City on Monday night. One was the evacuation of 500 parents, students and other honorees attending an awards ceremony at Midwest City High School

The other was the tornado.

Left in its wake was a city without power but loaded with debris and five deaths. Midwest City had not suffered a serious tornado in the past half-century.

For the 500 at Midwest City High School, the school's jazz band was just finding its groove, old friends were embracing, and the fun was just beginning. Principal Rick Bachman was at the lectern. His calm voice belied his concern when he made the announcement.

"The band reminds us of the music on the titanic, but we don't want to be like the Titanic, so let's quietly and orderly leave this building and walk over to the basement of the field house."

At table after table, smiles dissolved into quizzical looks as Bachman went on.

"We have just received word that a tornado has been spotted on the city's west side, so just to be safe, let's move on to the field house."

While some guests could not be deterred from their $8 dinners, most of the 500 did exactly as the principal asked.[12]

Possibly the best examples of modern-day storytelling techniques that can be used by nonfiction writers to create engaging and magnetic reading can be found in a story that began as a nonfiction magazine piece in the early 1990s, was later expanded into a best-selling book, and wound up a movie. The story has been referenced elsewhere in this book, and it is Sebastian Junger's neoclassic, *The Perfect Storm*.[13] The writing in this book is so good that I have used it as a supplementary textbook in some of my university journalism courses I teach. Learning by example and subsequent discussion of the techniques used by the writer is a wonderful way for students to learn. And this story, about the six ill-fated crewmembers of the commercial fishing boat, the Andrea Gail, is full of spectacular writing example. Let me share a few here, and talk about what makes them so engaging and such good examples of what Harrington would call intimate journalism.

A soft rain slips down through the trees, and the smell of ocean is so strong it can almost be licked off the air. Trucks rumble along Rogers Street and men in t-shirts stained with fish blood shout to each other from the decks of boats. Beneath them the ocean swells up against the black pilings and sucks back down to the barnacles.

Beer cans and old pieces of styrofoam rise and fall, and pools of spilled diesel fuel undulate like huge iridescent jellyfish. The boats rock and creak against their ropes and seagulls complain and hunker down and complain some more.

Across Rogers Street and around the back of the Crow's Nest, through the door and up the cement stairs, down the carpeted hallway and into one of the doors on the left, stretched out on a double bed in room number 27 with a sheet pulled over him, Bobby Shatford lies asleep.

He's got one black eye.[14]

Wow! What a way to sweep the unsuspecting reader into a modern-day true saga of men and the sea. Talk about descriptive writing that literally transports you and your imagination to the scene of a fateful event. Notice how Junger gets his descriptive effect largely with the telling vignettes— the details—of the town of Gloucester, Massachusetts. Notice how he expresses them largely with nouns and strong verbs, not so much with adjectives, and always with a preference for the shorter—rather than the longer—words and sentences. And notice how the underlying mood of the scene comes shining through without hammering the reader over the head with it. The lessons are clear and many: If you choose the right scene and do an accurate description of it, adjectives are often just unnecessary baggage. Less is usually more when it comes to writing and the expression of details and mood.

The very first sentence of this passage—probably the strongest sentence—contains only one adjective—"soft"—and it is a good one at that. It describes how the rain feels as well as looks. But the nouns and the verbs carry the load, assisted by some nice descriptive analogies, similes, and verbs. Among the strong, descriptive verbs used are "slips," "Licked," "rumble," "stained," "shout," "swells," "sucks," "undulate," "rock," "creak," "complain," and "hunker." If I were to pick one writing element that can deliver a knockout punch or miss the mark entirely, that would be the verb. And Junger uses the precise, short, descriptive verb to perfection in this passage. Lesser verbs—possibly more neutral ones—could have been used and might have been adequate, but these verbs deliver a lot more bang for the buck. You can actually see, hear, and feel the action through them.

Among the visual descriptions painted by Junger's words and expressions are: "...it can almost be licked off the air;" "...undulate like huge iridescent jellyfish;" and the allusion of seagulls complaining. Still another technique that adds freshness and immediacy to the story is telling it in the present tense.

Finally, notice the effect that the five-word closing paragraph has: "He's got one black eye." That's a great teaser for what's coming.

In short this passage helps you see, hear and feel what is going on at this time and in this seaside setting of Gloucester. And it contrasts the placidity and routine of the town's everyday life with the tumult that is about to come.

Starting to get your emotions revved up about this unfolding drama? And is it because of hyping and sensationalism, or just pure reporting and concise, descriptive writing? What's he doing here that is so magnetic? A few things seem obvious, and some not so. One obvious thing is that Junger is not afraid to take risks with his writing. That's good. Writer Maxwell Perkins once counseled, "You have to throw yourself away when you write."[15] Said another way, a good writer must be willing to take risks and take the consequences, good or bad, of his or her creativity. That's how new ground is broken; that is how Pulitzers are won, best-sellers are made, and that is how readers are engaged to the point of being mesmerized.

A second passage from Junger shows the detail at work in going intimate with an important character in the story, a Coast Guard rescuer who is dumped into the Atlantic when his helicopter fails:

Spillane doesn't remember the moment of impact, and he doesn't remember the moment he first realized he was in the water. His memory goes from falling to swimming with nothing in between. When he understands he is swimming, that is all he understands. He doesn't know who he is, why he is there, or how he got there. He has no history and no future; he is just a consciousness at night in the middle of the sea.

A person who has lost all four levels of consciousness, right down to their identity, is said to be "alert and oriented times zero." When John Spillane wakes up in the water, he is alert and oriented times zero. His understanding of the world is reduced to the fact that he exists; nothing more.[16]

Again we see a passage sure to elicit some reader emotion and adrenaline without having the writer veer at all from the details of the scene in front of him, as told to him by his source through some incisive interviewing. Rick Bragg says he is often asked how he gets the details and descriptiveness of his stories. He replies simply, "Somebody told me."[17] He believes that so much that he made it the title of his second book, an anthology of some of his best stories from the pages of the *Times*. In that book's introduction, Bragg explains:

Thank God for talkers. I grew up at the knee of front-porch talkers, of people who could tell a story and make you believe you had been there, right there, in the path of the bullet or the train, in the warm arms of a new mother, in the teeth of a mean dog. The men, sometimes dog drunk, sometimes flush with religion but always alight with the power of words, could make you feel the breath of the arching blade as it hissssssed past their face on the beer joint floor, could make you taste the blood in your mouth from the fist that had smashed into their own, could make you hear the loose change in the deputy's pocket as he ran, reaching for them, just steps behind...I owe those storytellers, all of them, because without them I would have no skills, no foundation, no accent, no voice. Their blood had trickled down to Alabama from a lot of places, from Ireland and Germany and France, mixing along the way with that of the Cherokee and Creek, finally pooling here. A drop from that pool is in every story I have ever written for wages...I took that borrowed ability and did some things with it, even made a living from it.[18]

Bragg here is simply echoing in concise, eloquent fashion what other great writers and editors have said for years. Be yourself in your writing, find your own voice, and go with it. Write about what interests you and don't be afraid to tell it in your own way. One such writing coach who encourages this approach is Chip Scanlan, director of writing programs at the Poynter Institute of Media Studies. In an essay entitled, "Do The Writing Only You Can Do," Scanlan said his best stories in years as a newspaper reporter and freelance magazine writer were those "commissioned by me."[19]

Many people say they want to write, but they don't know what to write about. Looking back at the stories I am proudest of, I can detect a central fact about each of them. They are pieces that only I could have written. That realization led me to a rule I try to live by: Do the writing only you can do... Every writer has a territory, a landscape of experience and emotional history unique to them. Like any landscape, there are safe havens and dangerous places. I could easily write a light-hearted piece about being the father of three girls. But the topic that needed exploring was my darker side: my temper with my kids. The essay I wrote begins with this painful scene:

It's late at night, and I'm screaming at my kids again. Yelling at the top of my lungs at three little girls, lying still and terrified in their beds. Like a referee in a lopsided boxing match, my wife is trying to pull me away, but I am in the grip of a fury I am unwilling to relinquish. "And if you don't get to sleep right now," I shout, "there are going to be consequences you're not going to like!"[20]

Some of my friends cautioned me against publishing this piece: people might get the wrong idea about me. But writing it has helped me understand myself [remember Joan Didion's comment, "I write entirely to find out what I'm feeling..."] and, more important, to understand my family better. Judging from the letters and phone calls I've received from readers grateful to see a painful issue in their life aired publicly, it's helped others too. Explore a dangerous region of your writer's territory by writing a piece nobody can write but you.[21]

Back to the third passage from Junger about Coast Guard diver John Spillane: Again, the present tense ("doesn't remember," "understands,") adds immediacy and a breathless quality to the piece. While it doesn't work for all stories, especially breaking news stories told in more traditional formats, it's not bad for narrative, and that is the form this story is told in.

One technique that works in this passage is the use of repetition for effect. So in the first sentence, "remember" is repeated in successive phrases, and then a variation of it (memory) is used in the second sentence. It is not redundancy because each use of the word describes a different memory. In the third sentence, the technique is used again as "understands" is repeated for effect. A sentence later, "no history" and "no future" are similar repeated phrases. Then, in the second paragraph, the key phrase "alert and oriented times zero" is repeated for effect.

Also in this passage you have the use of compound sentences joined by semi-colons instead of conjunctions. This gives a sense of more equality of content and impact of both phrases in these sentences. So you get, "He has no history and no future; he is just a consciousness at night in the middle of the sea." And, "His understanding of the world is reduced to the fact that he exists; nothing more." This construction also allows the second phrase to explain or summarize, or amplify on the first. But the semicolon is a softer break than a colon and it creates a more subtle effect in the mind of the reader than the colon would. So technically, although you could use a colon in these two sentences instead, you probably wouldn't want to.

There are a lot of grammar and stylistic guidelines and techniques at work in Junger's writing, but it is all geared to produce not just a factual description of the people and events that made up the Andrea Gail saga, but also to produce a contextual and mood-setting description. Often it is this latter description that settles longer into the mind and heart of the reader and gives the story its greatest impact, especially over time. And there is absolutely nothing fake, misleading, or sensational about such descriptive work. You are still dealing in the arena of facts and accuracy; you are just producing a larger picture of the people and event, even as you delve more intimately into both. And you do it often by using less— not more—verbiage.

Think you can't deliver concise, engaging detail that sucks readers into your copy? Wrong. And that is especially wrong if you are dealing with a question or issue that is almost universal among people. In writing *The Perfect Storm,* for example, how could you not write about the process of drowning, which is obviously going to be the fate of these six crewmen? Don't you think your readers have ever wondered what it must be like to drown? Think you can explain it without researching it and then taking time to make that explanation enticing and shorter, rather than longer and rambling? Junger deals with this question in his book, and writes about it engagingly and in detail.

In talking to a large group of reporters recently I made the comment often heard and too little understood: "When it comes to writing, less is more." After I finished, a reporter challenged me asking, "Why do you think that's true? Isn't detail still important in stories?" That exchange started me thinking more about this adage than ever before. First, the fact that so many superior writers have championed less give it face-value validity. Consider the following Freudian quips from these writers:

- Robert Louis Stevenson once noted, "There is but one art: to omit."
- Robert Browning said it more succinctly in that phrase we use today: "Less is more."
- Blaise Pascal said to a friend, "I have only made this letter rather long because I have not had time to make it shorter."

- Rabbi Israel Salanter once noted, "Writing is one of the easiest things; erasing is one of the hardest."
- And Isaac Bashevis Singer concluded, "The waste basket is a writer's best friend."

Beyond these testimonials lies this simple fact: The shorter, complete story will be read more often than the longer, complete story. The long story contains no inherent virtue over the shorter. If both are equally complete in content and meaning, why not go for the shorter one? That is exactly what has made Robert James Waller a best-selling author and a rich man. Whatever literary critics may think of *The Bridges of Madison County* and now his epilogue, *A Thousand Country Roads*, the fact remains the reading public loved the first with a passion that kept it on the *New York Times* Bestseller List for many months. Its runaway success was turned into a top box-office draw with Clint Eastwood and Merrill Streep, and the sequel, *A Thousand Country Roads*, made it to Number 5 on the *Times* Bestseller List its first week of distribution in the spring of 2002. And neither book hits the 200-page mark in length. Some fans felt it took less time to read *Bridges* than to see the movie. Descriptive and poignant? Yes, say hundreds of thousands of readers. Lengthy? No.

Tight, punchy, crisp, clear stories are read more often than loosely written stories loaded with flowery, ambiguous phrases. But when you hear, "Less is more," understand it refers to the dysfunctional material in a sentence, paragraph, or story. It does not simply celebrate brevity for its own sake. Rather, it is selective brevity that makes an unnecessarily long story better by making every word and phrase functional. Of course story detail is highly important, but it should be functional detail. Select only the detail that can stand for a larger picture or larger meaning, or evoke an appropriate emotional response from the reader or viewer.

Famed newspaper consultant Edmund Arnold has explained that story elements are either functional or dysfunctional. They either help or hinder the reader in moving through copy. Although Arnold was referring more to newspaper design elements than to writing itself, the adage holds true for both. No element of writing is really neutral in the sense of having no effect on readability of a story or portion of a story. It either helps the reader glide through a story or it acts as an impediment that can range in difficulty from a large boulder in the road to deep sandy footing underfoot.

The idea is to let the length of your copy match the length of your purpose. If you are telling a simple love story as Waller did, you don't need 400 pages. If, however, you are telling a saga of the Old West spanning a year or more, you may be writing *Lonesome Dove*, and you may need 1,000 pages because of the various sub-plots you have going and because of the sweep of the larger focus. But sometimes stories run long simply because the writer lacks a single focus for the piece and does try to cover too much territory. Sticking to a single theme and focus should automatically shorten copy. It will also heighten reader interest. It has been said that a carefully prepared and penetrating look at a single twig is far better than a lengthy essay on the whole tree. Create a deeper understanding of the twig, and you are more likely to develop more understanding of the tree.

The narrower your story's theme, the greater the chance you have to achieve impact on the reader and depth in the story itself. And the more likely you will come up with something truly profound and significant in meaning. Remember it is easier for the mind to focus on and remember a single focus than multiple ones. This is one reason why anecdotal and scene-setting leads are so good. They focus on someone doing something or some singular scene that a reader can easily grasp and envision in her mind's eye. It is a technique that filmmakers have used for decades: Deliver the close-up shot and you will deliver more drama than the medium or long shot.

How do practicing journalists feel about using the narrative style of reporting? Many seem to love it, especially for the right kinds of stories. Others are not so sure. They wonder if the old way isn't better; if the inverted pyramid isn't the best format for a news story. In 1998, Berrin Beasley, a journalism educator at the University of Southern Mississippi, published a story looking at journalists' attitudes toward narrative writing. In it, Beasley found reporters and editors from Gulf-area newspapers see a need for more narrative writing and think the changeover to this more descriptive form of writing is possible for daily journalists. In her study she notes a previous case study done by Georgia Greene that concluded:

The newspaper industry may be destroying itself by refusing to acknowledge that traditional newswriting conventions, such as fact organization, block paragraphs, and choppy sentences, make for difficult reading for the typical newspaper consumer. Green's case study of newswriting comprehensibility led her to the conclusion that while the inverted pyramid style may be beneficial to the minority of readers who prefer to skim for information, the inverted pyramid is a hindrance to most readers. She concluded that the pattern for writing stories should be overhauled, suggesting that new writing styles would increase reader comprehension.[22]

Greene notes that same conclusion was reached about 15 years later—in the mid 1990s—by the Literacy Committee of the American Society of Newspaper Editors in cooperation with the Poynter Institute for Media Studies, the *St. Petersburg Times*, and the University of Wisconsin-Madison.

In assessing journalists' attitudes toward narrative writing, Greene's study found:[23]

- All respondents agreed the narrative style is appropriate in the news section, "to a certain degree, which varied depending on the person interviewed."
- When the story focuses on a person, or people, or when there is drama or the event is compelling, most journalists felt the narrative is okay.
- Almost all agreed that the narrative style is not appropriate for first-run, breaking news stories. The reason? Most felt the narrative just does not give important information quickly enough for the reader who wants to know what happened.
- The most frequently mentioned barrier to narrative writing was lack of time. Respondents felt it takes more time to research and write the narrative piece, whereas the inverted-pyramid story just sort of rolls out of the average journalist in much less time.
- Space constraints came in second as a barrier to narrative writing, since it takes more space to tell a narrative story.
- Ranking third as a barrier, interestingly enough, was the journalists' writing ability. Many respondents felt that although anyone can write in the inverted-pyramid style, it takes a real writer to produce an effective narrative piece.

## SUMMARY

I have devoted a lot of attention in this chapter to the way stories are told and crafted by journalists. Some readers might ask, "I thought this was a book about reporting perspectives and the emotions involved in stories. I didn't know it was a textbook on writing." The fact is, the book is both and it must be. While a reporter may be vulnerable to emotional tugs in witnessing an event first-hand or spending time interviewing those who lived a tragedy, the reader's emotional reaction will depend on the way the story of that event or that person is written. They couldn't be there themselves to witness it and they rely on the wisdom and talent of the journalist to transport them there accurately. Even many talented journalists—like the oft-mentioned Joan Didion—get an emotional charge out of reading their own writing. It is much like the person who keeps a journal will get more of an emotional and sense-making jolt out of the copy they themselves wrote about what they themselves witnessed or experienced. This is one of the rewarding side benefits of being a journalist, in fact.

The best journalism is not simply a process of recording facts. Official minutes of a governmental meeting, or the official transcript of a court case will do that. This doesn't make anyone want to actually read those minutes or those transcripts, however. I once had a reader come in off the street and strongly urge our newspaper to do just that: run the minutes of the city council meeting instead of writing our own story about it. He was upset about the way our city hall reporter represented comments made in the meeting. His feeling was reporters are too vulnerable in editing comments and events of the meeting and sorting out what is important and what isn't. "Just run the official minutes!" he shouted. "Let the reader have it all!" My reaction was then as it is now: Very few people—if any—would be motivated to read those boring minutes.

Earlier in the book, I mentioned the idea that reporting is inseparable from interpretation. I still believe that, so I believe not interpreting events or not crafting a story of them in a particular style are not options. As reporters and writers, we will interpret everything—define "tall" by what we consider "short" and the like. The best writers will eschew the standard story structure formula and shoot for painting outside the lines in order to bring a more accurate, precise, and appropriate design to the project of describing reality. And if a journalist must bring all his or her senses to bear on that project—including the emotional punch he or she gets from witnessing that reality—then so be it.

Maybe more journalists need to live on the edge a little more and be willing to experience Steinbeck's feeling of holding fire in their hands. It should make the job much more enjoyable and enlightening for all concerned.

## NOTES

1. Walt Harrington, *Intimate Journalism: The Art and Craft of Reporting Everyday Life* (Thousand Oaks, Calif.: Sage, 1997), xix–xx.

2. Ibid., xi.

3. Ibid.

4. Ibid., xii.

5. Ibid., xx.

6. Ibid.

7. Rick Bragg, "A Thief Dines out, Hoping Later to Eat in," *New York Times*, 19 May 1994, reprinted in *Somebody Told Me* (Tuscaloosa: University of Alabama Press, 2000), 33.

8. Barry Bearak, "Visions of Holiness in Lubbock," *Los Angeles Times*, 18 November 1990, 1A.

9. Jim Willis and Simone Notter, "Fall of the Wall Saluted," *Daily Oklahoman*, 10 November 1999, 1.

10. Don Fry, "Getting Real People into Newswriting," handout, Poynter Institute's National Writers Workshop, Portland, Oregon, April 1999.

11. Ibid.

12. Jim Willis, "Killer Storm Spared Midwest City Crowd," *Daily Oklahoman*, 4 May 1999, 13.

13. Sebastian Junger, *The Perfect Storm* (New York: Harper Perennial, 1997).

14. Ibid., 5.

15. Robert I. Fitzhenry, ed., *The Harper Book of Quotations*, 3rd ed. (New York: Harper-Collins, 1993), 491–495.

16. Junger, *The Perfect Storm*, 188.

17. Bragg, "A Thief Dines out," 1.

18. Ibid.

19. Chip Scanlan, "Do the Writing Only You Can Do," an essay for the Poynter Institute of Media Studies, St. Petersburg, Florida, August 1996, available at www.poynter.org/research, 1.

20. Ibid., 2.

21. Ibid.

22. Berrin Beasley, "Journalists' Attitudes toward Narrative Writing," *Newspaper Research Journal,* 19. no. 1 (Winter 1998): 78.

23. Ibid., 84–85.

# Chapter 6

# Writers and Their Writing

So there you sit, an aspiring journalist—or possibly even a practicing one—staring at a blank computer page document. You are ready to pounce on that page and bare your literary soul to the reader or viewer, when a nagging question swells up inside you: Who am I writing for, anyway, and what does he or she expect of me? Will they like my work or won't they, and what can I do to make my writing irresistible to them? With such ponderings, you have entered the realm of writer/reader/ viewer dynamics. It may seem like an abstract realm to nonwriters, but it is a very real place for serious journalists. What can be said about the relationship of a writer to his or her reader or viewer?

For starters, there is definitely a kind of unwritten contractual agreement between you and him or her. It is your responsibility to make the writing informative, revealing, and entertaining. It is your reader's responsibility to take time to read or listen to it. There are some keys that can help bring this contract to fruition, and there are some things you can do to derail the whole relationship. Let's start by looking at the nature of writing, as journalists practice it, and what that means to the reader.

Of course it all starts with good grammar, but it goes way beyond that as Lauren Kessler and Duncan McDonald point out in their splendid writing guide, *When Words Collide:*

Consider the plight of the journalists. In the swirl of Information gathering, harried journalists are expected to extract, analyze and select items that will inform, stimulate, and entertain an equally harried and often distracted audience. If that isn't enough, communications specialists face another challenge: the correct, concise use of the language.[1]

In his essay, "Journalism: Understanding an Old Craft as an Art Form," G. Stuart Adams defines journalism as, "an invention for a form of expression used to report and comment in the public media on the events and ideas of the here and now."[2] As the earlier discussions in this book have pointed out, there is a variety of orientations and perspectives that journalists bring to their craft. No two individual journalists are likely to report the same story the same; each is more likely to construct his or her own personal frame. It's a way they use of expressing themselves and of telling stories. Some writers have studied their own motivations in writing and have come to some interesting conclusions.

Writer Joan Didion, for example, says, "I write entirely to find out what I'm thinking, what I'm looking at, what I see and what it means...When I talk about pictures in my mind, I am talking about images that shimmer around the edges. The shimmer is definitely there. You can't think too much about them. You just lie low and let the pictures develop...you try to locate the cat or dog or college student in the shimmer; you try to locate the grammar in the picture."[3]

I like that. For one thing, this craving to discover what you yourself are thinking and feeling by looking at what you have to say about the phenomenon, provides a rich motivation. It means our writing is not only a catharsis for our feelings but also is a form of self-analysis where we can actually see what we are thinking or feeling. If the concept of journaling has any merit at all in coming to understand yourself and deal with life, then journalists should know themselves better than anyone because—to writers like Didion—journaling is what they do for a living. They may convey the story differently than you might find in a person's journal or diary; they may delete the opinions and value statements—at least the overt ones—but still the writer's own perception comes through in that writing. And that perception can have a lot to say to a writer willing to analyze it as Didion does. For these souls, writing is a means of bringing Didion's shimmer into focus. It is akin to a far-sighted person seeing before-and-after takes of a page of writing, before and after they don their reading glasses. Once the glasses go on, the shimmer turns into something realizable that makes sense.

As an invention, journalism really is a product of the writer's imagination, both individually and culturally. This might trouble some people, especially those who feel journalism should be about reality and not fantasy. But calling the expressive form of journalism an invention doesn't mean the story must deviate from reality. As chapter 2 pointed out with many examples, it just means the writer approaches that reality in different ways; from different perspectives; with different writing techniques and structures. In fact, it is this imaginative form of expression that makes journalism so readable, or, conversely, it is a lack of imagination that makes it so boring. It is a form of expression wherein the imagination of the individual writer and his or her culture are revealed. So, as Adams notes, although individual writers speak individually in their journalism, they speak through a cultural form—usually a kind of story structure—they did not invent. Examples of these cultural forms would be the story formats of the inverted pyramid, or the so-called hour-glass structure.

So journalism emerges as a kind of template or a form of expression, just as a novel or narrative film are forms of expressions. In poetry, you have sonnets, epics, limericks, and free verse. In journalism you have news stories, sidebars, backgrounders, analyses, news features, columns, editorials, and reviews.

This imaginative aspect of journalism conjures up the subjective aspect of a journalist's objectivity. Again, subjectivity is an observational process influenced by the subject viewing the object. As such, it is impossible to think of any observation made by a human as being anything other than subjective. Adams notes:

Think about this: Imagining is the self making and recognizing images. So the world out there is composed of objective images like trees and chewing gum and elephants. But to express what we see to others who aren't there, we first have to form images and then, through language or other art forms, we crate imagery or snapshots of the objective world.[4]

A semanticist would say, "the map is not the territory." Journalist/philosopher Walter Lippmann talked about, "the world outside and the pictures in our head." He also talks of seeing versus defining and of how many people define before they see.

Another good thing about Didion's perspective is it portrays the journalist as lying low and letting the images develop on their own, away from the spotlight that the journalist too often represents. How many personas and events are altered when the obtrusive reporter and/or the lights and cameras show up? Isn't this what judges wrestle with in deciding whether to allow cameras in the courtroom? Aren't they really dealing with the issue of how candid and objective things will be when the lawyers start playing to the cameras? A low-lying journalist is a good thing when it comes to letting the action speak for itself, at least as much as that is possible. Even when a journalist might become part of the action, he or she only does it to get closer to the core of things. Rarely do they make a show of being involved as they want to focus on the real newsmakers.

And again, while this reporting and later reconstruction of events is taking place, the good journalist has the reader in the back of his or her mind, seeing himself as a representative of that reader and asking the questions he or she might ask were they there themselves.

Joseph Conrad, writer of captivating sea tales and adventure stories, has told protégé's, "My task, which I am trying to achieve is, by the power of the written word, to make you hear, to make you feel—It is, before all, to make you see."[5] That aspect of writing, born of a desire to transport the reader to the scene beyond their reach, can be seen in the following story excerpt about an on-site memorial service two weeks after the Alfred P. Murrah Federal Building bombing in Oklahoma City in April of 1995:

You stand on Fifth Street in the shadow of what once was the Alfred P. Murrah Federal Building. There is a ceremony under way, but you can't take your eyes off the nine-story carcass in front of you.

For one of just a few days since its bombing, the afternoon sun bathes much of the area. Hundreds of search-and-rescue workers come to pay their respects. They remember those 167 who died inside its walls, including the two women's bodies yet uncovered and nurse Rebecca Anderson who lost her life during an early rescue effort.

Six of those lost are still unidentified.

And they remember the many who did so much in trying to save the savable and locate the lost.

On this Friday, it was time for rescuers, volunteers, and even journalists to remember and to mourn.

You look up and see this monument of man's inhumanity to man; its hollowed-out section of floors, and the rubble pile remaining below. Yet you also know you are staring straight into a tower of love and self-sacrifice.

Everywhere you look you see flowers, wreaths, Teddy bears and hand-painted signs of thanks. A rose juts its dark red head out of an orange highway cone that is wrapped with duct tape and which appears to have been kicked more than once by a frustrated fireman.

Another rose dangles from a camera tripod belonging to a Reuters TV news photographer. Elsewhere, two fatigues-clad National Guardsmen—like many of their comrades—bow their heads and clutch rose stems behind their backs.

There are those who insist that, in the battle between the eye and the ear, the eye wins every time. That seems true here today. There is so much to see, so much to take in. There is so much to remember.[6]

Back to Adams' definition of journalism: Another aspect of it is its public nature. Said another way, journalism is created for public consumption. That is both tricky and risky—as well as potentially very rewarding—for the writer. The poet Edna St. Vincent Millay once noted just how risky writing is when she drew the comparison of putting oneself into print as being like appearing willfully in public with your pants down.[7] The reason? A writer must expose himself or herself to a group of strangers and put his or her work out there for public critiquing of everything from grammar, to style, to logic. Many writers shiver at the prospect of releasing their writing to the public for just that reason. It is akin to the stage fright a performer or actor might feel just before going on stage. Even the most veteran of entertainers can feel vulnerable. For example, late in his career singer/actor Frank Sinatra told TV talk show host Larry King he still felt flutters of apprehension during the first few moments of each concert he did. The same is true for many writers. Witness what Jon Franklin had to say about releasing his classic story, "Mrs. Kelly's Monster," to the public:[8]

Then I got scared. It was like stage fright. I knew I was going to put it out there and call a lot of attention to myself. This one was going to move people...To be a fine writer, intelligence is important. But I think the real game is to perceive reality correctly. The writing part is technically how we do it, the lens through which we see. But you've got to be able to see reality when it's not what you expected, and when you know it's not what other people want to see. You've got to be able to stare right at it. It takes courage to let yourself go blank and see what really is there.

Because journalism is for public consumption, Adams notes that its voice and vocabulary are colored by purposive or didactic responsibilities such as explicitness, an absence of obscure allusions, and by the absence of specialized jargon that only a few readers might understand. Journalism instructors and editors are constantly admonishing their writers to humanize the jargon or stilted language used by lawyers, police officers, doctors, and educators and put their thoughts into everyday layman's English.

It is this public consumption aspect that mandates writers write at a level easily understood by a cross-section of readers. Over the years, many readability formulas have cropped up that measure the ease with which a particular piece of writing can be read. Most work off an index that either equates with an age or a year in school the reader should have completed in order to read the writing easily. Writing coach Jack Hart has noted in an article entitled, "Writing to be Read:"

Newspapers consistently publish major stories above the reading level of most potential newspaper buyers. Small wonder, then, that newspapers reach only half of the nation's households.

Don't believe it? Just look at the facts: only about two in five American adults have completed college. About the same proportion have graduated from high school but never went any further. About one in five never finished high school. The average educational attainment level is 12.7 years.

Newspaper reading is a leisure activity. Most subscribers read the paper because they want to; not because they have to. Just because somebody can read something doesn't mean they want to. In fact, readability experts say most of us prefer reading about three grade levels under our actual educational level. By that standard, publications aimed at a general audience should strive for scores of about ten.

Clearly we have a problem.[9]

Readability formulas are generally based on average sentence length and the percentage of words with three or more syllables. Both the Gunning Fog Index and the Flesch-Kincaid readability tests do that. They both produce an index number that equates with the last grade in school a reader should have completed in order to easily understand a piece of writing. So if the index produced is a 12, then the reader should have completed his or her senior year of high school to easily understand the passage of writing.

Here's how the Gunning Fog Index would work:

1. Take a sample of your writing, ranging from 100–150 words. Stop at the first period after the 100-word mark. That may be 101 or it may be 149 or anywhere in between.

2. Count the number of sentences in the passage and divide that number into the passage length to get the average sentence length, in words. If you have a passage size of 100 words containing 10 complete sentences, your average sentence length is 10 words.

3. Count the number of words containing three or more syllables. Divide the entire passage length into that number of words to get the percentage of difficult words. So if you have a sample of 100 words and 13 of them are difficult you would divide 100 into 13 and get a percentage of .13. Turn that number into a whole number by dropping the percentage point, to continue to the next step.

4. Add the results of steps 2 and 3, and multiply by .6. In this example, you add 10 and 13, get 23 and multiply by .6 to get a fog index of 13.8.

So, in order to understand that passage easily, the reader should have had at least a year of college.

Of course your fog index might vary greatly depending on the demographics of your readership. The *Boston Globe,* for example, has a fairly literate and well-educated readership. Several years ago, a readability test on this newspaper showed a fog index of over 15, equating with completion of the junior year of college. The *Globe*'s crosstown rival, on the other hand, showed a much lower index. The *Boston Herald,* a tabloid aimed at a wider array of demographics than the *Globe,* showed a fog index of 8 during this same test. That equates with an eighth-grade education.

Finally, according to Adams's definition of journalism, this writing is related to the here and now. The world of journalism, unlike the world of history for example, is the real world as a whole comprehended under the category of the present. Certainly a knowledge of the past is helpful in creating a more accurate picture of the story, but it is a story written about something whose impact is felt here and now.

A news story differs in some respects from a novel, and in other respects there is strong similarity, depending on how the journalist may structure the story. It is interesting to note how the philosophies behind these differing story structures have evolved. Historically, news stories are event-oriented and have been defined narrowly and in terms of conflict or consequences or human interest or prominence of the key characters or supporting cast in the stories. Also historically, fiction is more concerned with the inner lives of the actors in the stories, whereas a journalist usually stops at the outer limits of the event he or she is reporting about. Another way of looking at it, as Adams does, is to say that the novelist must suspend the blur of events to make passion—or the intensities of the human heart—the focus for readers' contemplation. Conversely, in a real sense, journalism is the blur; it is about the events that the mysteries of passion or a competition of love or hate produce.

Now, within the world of journalism there is both the hard news story and the soft feature story. At one time there was a fairly sharp dividing line between the two of these forms of expression. Traditionally, news has been seen as something different from a story's subject. Subjects are one thing, while the news is another. Adams uses the example of a story about the rainforest. The rainforest can be thought of as the story's subject, while the fact it is in trouble is the news. The motive of the feature—sometimes called the human-interest story—is to divert attention from the larger issue to focus on the emotions stirred by that issue or event.

Today, this line between news and features is much more blurred. Many news stories are now told in narrative formats that begin through an extended anecdote about an individual caught up in the larger event or issue. That anecdote may describe how the person is coping with the situation; how she feels about it, and so forth. Formerly, that would have been the stuff of feature stories. But no more. As another chapter points out, the concept of storytelling has softened the lines or boundaries between news and feature stories. In today's news story, the blur of events is often suspended to show the inner conflicts of key characters in that story or to show the emotional aspect or impact of the story.

Two decades ago, writing coach Robert Leon Baker advised journalists of the need to romance their readers. Baker warned of leaving the reader out of the equation when it comes to developing a story. He advised adding the concept of reader relations to the lexicon of phrases like consumer relations, employee relations, and government relations. Often when I think about Baker's good counsel, I'm reminded of a survey of editors I did years ago. The survey asked editors to rate a series of stories on how newsworthy they thought they were, then to rate the same stories on how newsworthy the readers thought they were. The differences in the ratings were startling, and I will discuss them later in this chapter. The point here is to note how one editor responded when asked if it bothered him that his rating scheme was dramatically different from what he perceived his average reader's to be. The editor responded, "It is a conflict of interest for me to worry about the reader's desires."[10] I had trouble believing the response when I saw it then, although I understand what he's getting at, and I still have trouble believing it today. That idea is the antithesis of romancing your reader or of believing there is a sort of unwritten, contractual agreement between the writer and reader.

On the opposite pole, Baker writes:

We not only want our readers to look at our publications, we want them to stop a moment and read. We want them to digest mentally what they read. And we want them—if necessary—to be moved a little by what they have read and the new insight they have gained. It is not easy to get that message across. They say that you can send a message around the world in a split second, yet it may take years to project one simple idea through a quarter-inch of skull. . . . It should keep you asking yourself, "Is anybody reading what we print?" Is there an "average reader" for us to seek out and use as an editorial target? Since every human being is a distinct individual unlike any other human being, we don't think this approach is a good one. How can one possibly chart the yearnings of each reader from a mythical average? How can one catalog the degrees of hate, vanity, fear, envy, selfishness, superstition, and sentimentality that exists in each person? But we can know through research findings in the behavioral sciences "what makes people tick" in general. Let's apply some of these generalities to our readers.[11]

And the following are some of the applications to which Baker alludes about what makes people tick.

- Readers yearn for a measure of fame. They want success, recognition, appreciation, even praise when they think it is due. When your readers excel, take note and write about it.

- Readers want more of the good things of life. They would like an income that would let them live in a bit more luxurious manner. Write about ways people find of making that happen.

- Readers want love, security, and a happy home. Readers want some assurance that their job will last and their income continue. They want to merit the love and respect of their families, their relatives, co-workers, and friends. Look for stories that address these needs.

- Readers want adventure. They want to occasionally escape from more mundane affairs, even doing so vicariously through the adventures of others.

- Readers want to lead long, healthy lives. The interest in medical news has never been stronger, especially since the Baby Boomers are now well into their fifties. This interest also means readers are interested in stories about risks they may face in their day-to-day lives that threaten their personal security.

- Our readers want to believe they are different. They want to feel they are unique and special in some ways and worthy of respect in all ways.

On the opposite side of this list are things writers can do to alienate reader affections.[12] In some ways, of course, that can be done by ignoring the list just discussed. But there are other ways as well.

- Underestimate your readers and their ability to spot stories with holes in them or stories that don't make sense. Some writers hide their own superficial knowledge of a subject by resorting to generalities or flippant writing.

- Forget about creative approaches to stories and write in consistent structures and vocabulary in ways that will sterilize your stories in the interest of keeping them objective. This is the wrong way to attain objectivity, which, of course, deals with facts and not so much with writing techniques. Instead, keep your copy vibrant with new life, new style, and new facts. Tell your stories in terms of people, and use storytelling pictures. Show people in action and write visually.

- Put blinders on when developing story ideas. Don't color outside the lines in terms of finding new and different subject matter for your stories. Create a situation where, when the reader sees your byline, he or she will automatically know what you're writing about because you are so predictable in your subject matter.

- Write your stories in a complex and obfuscating manner, hiding profound truths beneath a mountain of rhetoric. Instead, think about letting those profundities arise more easily from simple, clear and concise language.

- Tamper with the facts, and never, never validate the facts. This will lose you more readers than dandruff flakes, and it will also put you squarely into the realm of fiction writing while masquerading as a non-fiction journalist.

In his essay, Baker concludes that editors as well reporters should always be thinking about the reader. He writes:

It has been said that "the first requisite for any writer is the understanding heart." We can apply that requisite to ourselves as editors. We, too, perhaps more than writers, need an understanding heart, so that we will think about our reader on every word we consider, every picture we scan, every personal contact we make.[13]

For some time, marketers and even many editors have known that if they don't take the reader into consideration when developing and preparing their stories, a number of negative things can happen. The most serious of these, of course, is losing the reader altogether. When readers perceive their hometown newspaper staff has become so arrogant as to distance themselves from readers' needs and desires, the loyalty factor will drop off sharply. They are under no obligation to continue subscribing to—or even reading—the newspaper when there are so many other information sources available. When you think about it, why should newspaper customers (readers) be any different from consumers of other products or services who will turn to competitors if they feel their needs are not being met by the manufacturer or service provider?

For most products in the marketplace, in fact, quality is improved when the consumer is taken more into consideration by the manufacturer. Why? Because consumers don't generally buy products that don't work or that fall apart, or that are too cumbersome to use. Innovations and improvements in manufacturing often come from listening to the consumer and hearing what applications they think are missing from the current product or service. Wouldn't the same be true for journalism? Wouldn't a newspaper or television newscast be improved by simply listening to the reader or viewer and attending to what they say they want to read in the paper or see on the newscast?

Not necessarily says researcher John McManus of Santa Clara University. In an article entitled, "Serving the Public and Serving the Market: A Conflict of Interest?" the researcher uses market theory microeconomics to test the assertion that serving the market helps insure that newspapers serve the public as well. McManus concludes:

The analysis concludes that news is a peculiar commodity—what economists call a "credence" good—that may invite fraud because consumers cannot readily determine its quality, even after consuming it. News, by definition, is what we don't yet know. Advertisers seek public attention for their products rather than public education about current events. Thus advertiser-supported news media, following market logic, compete not in a news market but in a larger market for public attention. This attention market may value entertainment more than information, leading to a conflict with journalism's norms of public service.[14]

McManus believes that market theory—or microeconomics—predicts that for most commodities, market forces push quality up and prices down. That creates wealth for both buyers and sellers.[15] But he notes two major flaws in the reasoning of those who assert that news media that do a good job serving the market also best serve the public and the implied mandate in the First Amendment:

- The assumption that news media serve a news market at all. As his conclusion states, the media serve more a market for public attention than simply for news. A viewer who watches the evening newscast for entertainment, weather or sports, counts just as much on the Nielsen People Meter as a viewer who watches to be educated or informed. The same is true for newspapers and how they register in readership surveys.

- As for the second flaw, he suggests looking at four key assumptions underlying market theory: (A) both sides to the transaction—news corporations and consumers—act rationally to pursue their own interest; (B) both are able to evaluate the quality of the product and the market for it; (C) there is competition in the market; and (D) no negative "externalities"—social costs generated by the transaction—exist. He concludes that, "the more of these conditions that are violated and the more serious the violation, the greater the likelihood that one party will take advantage of the other or that society will be harmed.[16] In the case of the news media and the public, these assumptions are violated with regularity, he asserts.

Earlier I mentioned a survey of editors who rated a series of news stories and then rated them as they thought their readers might. The results are revealing about whether newspapers are staying close to their readers or not. How much do editors consider the desires of their readers when selecting and positioning stories? Does an editor's sense of news value correspond at all with his or her perceptions of the reader? Do the differences between the two senses of news value concern the editors?

These were the focal questions for a survey of 52 managing editors from daily newspapers around the country.[17] Answers indicate that differences in news judgment do exist—not just between editor and reader but also among editors themselves. In addition, few of the responding editors seemed overly concerned about those differences as they went about seeing the daily news agenda for their newspapers. Yet the results also showed a general similarity in judging which types of stories should be given higher news value ratings and which should be given lower ratings. It was the actual placement of stories on a 1–16 news value scale, and the editor's perception of how the readers would place them, that varied many times.

The fact that most editors did not seem unduly concerned with differences between their news sense and their perception of the reader's news sense is seen in the following sample of responses to the questions of why such differences might exist and whether the editors are bothered by them:

- "Editors realize the importance of news that may not be exciting reading. I'm not too worried about the differences. Some news is news people want to know; some they just need to know."
- "We have an obligation to report the news, not judge it by our likes and dislikes or by what we think people may or may not like." (This is an interesting response in that the editor seems to assume a story somehow makes its way into the newspaper automatically without an editor judging it worthy of publication and then slotting it for a particular place in the newspaper. Clearly, that would be an impossible phenomenon.)
- "Everyone perceives the importance of news differently. That's why we carry a variety of news stories."
- "I rank stories for a broad appeal; not for any specific interest group."
- "Editors should try to take a balanced look at what is interesting and meaningful. Individual readers look at only what is interesting." (An interesting response in light of the earlier comment about readers' perceptions of arrogance on the part of editors and also the warning from Robert Leon Baker about underestimating your readers.)

And then there is that interesting observation noted earlier:

- "It is a conflict of interest for me to worry about the reader's desires."

Only a few editors among the 52 said the difference in news judgments really concern them. Among these editors, the following responses surfaced:

- "Yes, the differences concern me. We have to be in step with the readers without sacrificing traditional press responsibilities."
- "Yes. Newspapers are far too heavily weighted to male views and interests, primarily because men control most newsroom policies." (That, by the way, came from a male editor.)

Some editors chided their readers for not having a better sense of news judgment:

- "Editors tend to look at the overall significance while readers are attracted by the immediate happening. Editors tend to feed readers what's good for them while readers read what actually interests them."
- "Readers are becoming interested in insignificant news, and their knowledge of really important matters is shallow." (Again, a reader's perception of editorial arrogance might find a mark in this editor. This is also a case of an editor lumping all kinds of readers—from occasional to avid—together in the same pool with similar characteristics.)

This survey was prompted by the rising interest in marketing research among newspaper executives and the inroads such marketing efforts have made on the once off-limits arena of editorial autonomy, if that ever existed at all. In this survey, managing editors were asked to rate 16 stories on a 1–16 news value scale, with 1 being a lead story and 16 the lowest-rated story. The stories were suggested by the following headlines:

- City Council Rezones East Side.
- $5,000 Taken in Bank Heist.
- Jamie Fiske, 5, Has Liver Transplant.
- Local Schools Adopt Minimum-Standard Testing Policy.
- Local Woman Alleges Rape by Two Teens.
- Medical Journal Study Sheds New Light on Cancer Causes.
- Sales Tax Receipts Up 10% for Downtown Merchants.
- You Can Beat the High Cost of Getting a Divorce.
- State Legislature Approves Hike in Funding for State Roads.
- Fire Destroys Home; Mother, Son Injured.
- Interest Rates Up 1.5% on CDs in Most Area Banks.
- President to Meet with Lebanese Leader over Beirut Crisis.
- Two New Members Elected to Local Alderman Board.
- Area Teacher has Harrowing Experience on Rome Trip.
- Computer Craze Likely to Continue.
- Jury Finds 3 Area Men Guilty of Manslaughter.

Some of the editors were asked to give their perception of an average male reader's rating, while the other editors were asked for their perception of female readers' ratings. Thirty-two of the respondents judged men's ratings, while 20 perceived women's ratings. Altogether, the survey was mailed to 100 managing editors on daily papers, 10,000 and above in circulation. The bulk of the responses—37—came from editors of dailies less than 50,000 in circulation. Of the 52 responses, 40 were from male editors and 12 from female editors.

Some of the more interesting survey findings were:

- Editors exhibited little uniformity in placement of the stories on the 1–16 ratings scale. For instance, only one-fourth of the editors rated the same story as the lead story, and fewer still cast votes for any of the other stories.
- The fire and testing policy stories emerged as the top two stories in the minds of just more than half of the editors.
- Of the five stories garnering the most votes in the minds of editors and their perceptions of readers' ratings, only two common stories emerged on each list: the fire and school testing-policy stories.
- Stories most editors rated in the top 25 percentile were the school testing policy, rezoning, fire, bank heist, liver transplant, and jury verdict.
- Stories most editors rated in the bottom 25 percentile were those on the computer craze, Rome trip, divorce, interest rates, and the president's meeting with Lebanese leaders.
- Stories most editors perceived their readers to rate in the bottom 25 percentile were the computer craze, Lebanese meeting, sales tax receipts, interest rates, and divorce advice.
- While 27 editors chose the rezoning story for a top 25 percentile story, only 14 editors said their readers would so pick it.
- While only 10 editors picked the rape story as a top 25 percentile story, only 14 said their readers would so pick it.
- While 15 editors picked the Lebanese story as a top 25 percentile story, 26 said their readers would.
- Several differences appeared between male and female editors in their respective ratings of stories and in their perceptions of how readers might rate them. For instance, just fewer than half of the male editors rate the divorce story as an upper-level piece, while none of the female editors did. Also, 54 percent of the male editors thought their readers would rate the rape story in the upper level, while only 30 percent of the female editors did. Further, 50 percent of the male editors felt their readers would rate the fire story as an upper-level piece, while 70 percent of the female editors thought the readers would.
- Female editors showed far more congruency between their own ratings and their perceptions of reader ratings than did male editors.

Overall, the results indicated that the responding editors share a concern for their own rights and abilities to select their newspaper's news agenda. It also showed they feel readers want more entertaining stories rather than significant ones, that the editors themselves have no common idea of the exact placement of the stories, that they hold several traditional stereotypes of men and women readers' tastes in news, and that women editors have more congruence between their sense of news value and their perception of their readers' news judgment.

A study done a decade later by a team of Ohio University researchers also looked at this subject of how well an editor can predict reader interest in news. The study looked at public preferences and editors' estimates of those preferences and revealed that many editors overestimate reader interest in crime, religion, the stock market, local business, and sports.[18] The study surveyed half of the Ohio daily newspapers of less than 50,000 circulation. All of the newspapers of 50,000 circulation and over were included. Some 46 newspapers were thus surveyed. The companion survey was done on 426 randomly selected Ohio adults, asking for their preference. Both surveys asked about interest in 11 different kinds of news. The topics included local religion, local health, local schools, local business, the stock market, local crime, the governor, the legislature, local young people, local older people, and high school sports.

Results showed that highest public interest was in local health, local schools, and young people. Most editors correctly assumed that the public would want this kind of news. For their part, however, editors correctly predicted the interest level of only one of the other eight kinds of news. That was coverage of the governor. There was much disagreement between editors and the public on the other seven kinds of news. The public wanted more coverage of the legislature and older people, but most editors predicted they would want the same amount of coverage. And most editors felt the public would prefer more crime coverage, and stories about religion, the stock market, local business, and high school sports. However, most of the public did not want more coverage of any of these types of stories. Instead they wanted the same amount of coverage.

The researchers concluded:

But the evidence of this study is that editors are not very good at estimating reader interest. While former journalists turned media critics may attack corporate newspapers for marketing the news, the results suggest that they probably aren't doing it very well because they can't estimate reader interest accurately. That the editors of larger papers were slightly better in predicting reader interest may lend support to (the) argument that modern business practices employed by larger newspapers produce papers that readers find more attractive.[19]

This whole discussion of how close a newspaper should stay to its readers leads us into the arena of how much the reader should influence the type of news agenda presented in the paper in the first place. This is the debate over marketing the news that has divided newsrooms across the country. Journalistic purists want the newsroom to remain a bastion of autonomy wherein only the trained journalists make decisions about what is news. Those decisions, the argument goes, should be based exclusively on the merits of the event or issue as a significant news or feature story. Others argue, however, that taking the reader's desires into account makes sense on a number of fronts. Not the least of these is that it would be nice to know the stories are being read by a large segment of the readership. Stories defined as significant by the editor, but unread by the news consumer (possibly just because they need to be written in a more engaging style), will produce no results in terms of trying to get a perceived wrong righted. It's the old argument that asks, if a tree falls in the woods and no one is around to hear it, does it make any noise?

But just how far does a newspaper's obligation to the general public go? We talk often, for instance, of the public's right to know and the public's need to know. But what about the public's want to know? Is the fascination with gossip and titillation within the scope of the daily newspaper's social obligation? Much of the newspaper industry has been acting as if it is. As newspapers continue to chase subscribers in a mass-circulation arena, they often must cater to the apathetic (industry researchers call them "marginal") readers. Why? Because often that is where the incremental growth for a newspaper will lie.

If newsroom budgets were unlimited, offering something for everyone might not be so questionable. The reality is the opposite, however. Newsroom budgets are tight and getting tighter. Whatever money goes toward the shadow of news is money taken away from the substance of news.

Several years ago, the Newspaper Association of America suggested newspapers could go for a Mass Appeal, Class Appeal, Individual Appeal, or Direct Appeal in their efforts to survive and prosper. We haven't heard much about this debate recently until a 1998 article surfaced in The *American Editor*, which is the official journal of the American Society of Newspaper Editors. That article made a strong appeal for the newspaper industry to avoid going for a Mass Appeal and, instead, to focus on a Class Appeal. That "class" was defined as those people interested enough in serious news to pay for it and read it.[20]

No one except monopoly-loving Wall Street appears happy with the current climate in newsrooms or the way much news is being defined and packaged now. The situation is full of irony. Industry research indicates that newspaper circulation is flat, even as reporters and editors grow weary over delivering a compromised brand of journalism designed to attract the larger audiences they are not getting.

In 1997 some 50 editors of top newspapers and academics making up the ASNE Ethics and Values Committee met at the *Philadelphia Inquirer* to study these twin factors in newspaper credibility. Much was said about gaining more credibility by focusing on the traditional standards of accuracy, fairness, depth, and balance. There was general reluctance among the editors to talk about what readers might want. That reluctance echoed the majority of editors from the 1987 study, discussed earlier in this chapter, who displayed a similar reluctance. Some dedicated editors at the 1997 symposium even suggested this ASNE credibility study should not be concerned with marketing considerations.

Some in the industry believe that, admirable as that thinking is, it belies what is common practice in the newspaper industry and it also belies the reality of the newspaper business. Responding to a recent survey on credibility, several top editors noted that credibility is a reader's issue, and not only a journalist's issue. The readers, this thinking goes, define whether a newspaper is credible. And readers may or may not use the same yardstick for measuring that credibility that a dedicated newspaper editor might. Many feel that, if journalists want to define credibility in their own terms, they will never do it while appealing to a mass-circulation market that is essentially a market for attention and not for news. In a market for attention, the person who buys the paper for the comics counts as much as one buying it for the news stories.

The option for the newspaper, of course, is to break off the chase and redefine its market, much as the magazine industry starting doing in the 1970s. After the giant, general-circulation magazines like *Look* and the original *Life* folded, the magazine industry moved ahead by charting a new course in targeting niche audiences. Today, magazines are stronger than ever. Most have simply redefined themselves as specialized magazines, aimed at specialized—or special-interest—audiences. The risk that magazines took was that circulation numbers could be sacrificed for circulation quality. And quality readers were defined as those with an intense level of interest in the magazine's subject matter and also its specialized advertisements. If that interest were strong enough, the argument went, then a smaller circulation base would suffice if the right advertising mix were found for the content. The argument proved correct, and the specialized magazine industry boomed and largely replaced what had been primarily a mass-circulation magazine market. And it is interesting that, among the leaders in the mass-circulation magazine market are news magazines such as *Time* and *Newsweek*. Who says you can't focus on news and still gain large audiences?

Of course, some newspapers have already moved in the direction of seeking more intense readers. The *New York Times,* the *Boston Globe,* and the *Wall Street Journal* are among them. Their uniqueness lies in targeting their market's most interested readers and giving them a solid news product. Yes, they also provide diversions along the way. But the main focus of the news hole is what most observers would term solid news. Marketing efforts directed at the marginal, apathetic readers seem to take backseat to the reader who wants to know what is happening in the city, state, nation, and world. Interesting, isn't it, that these are also three of the largest circulation newspapers in America? Associated with such readership is strong education, affluence, and community involvement. Coincidentally, these are just the factors most advertisers target as well.

The Class Appeal (a worse name than Focused Appeal) strategy often calls for aggressive pricing that would increase circulation rates while sustaining overall circulation declines of up to 25 percent. The readers who remain, however, would be the ones with the solid interest in news.

Does this translate to abandoning some readers and to pricing a newspaper beyond the reach of the ordinary American? Proponents of the Focused—or Class—Appeal strategy ask us to consider who is abandoning whom. This strategy targets those individuals interested enough in the news to read it. If an individual wants to avoid the news, then he or she is the one doing the abandoning, the argument goes. There is the analogy of the 6-year-old child who sometimes cries because she feels left out of a conversation between her parents at home. But all she must do to be included is to get involved in that chat. Ask a question or make a comment. Even just listen to the discussion. It is the same with marginal readers and non-readers, and proponents of the Class Appeal strategy say it is their responsibility to get involved.

Further, the argument goes, it is highly unlikely that a newspaper that targets news-hungry readers would abandon coverage of any market segments. Why? Because of the very nature of the curious readers they are serving. Focusing on significant news doesn't mean simply going high-brow and ignoring total segments of readers. And, as to pricing the newspaper beyond the level of people able to pay, we do live in the internet age in which anyone can go into a library and log onto any newspaper Web site in the world free of charge. And for those who want the traditional ink-on-paper product delivered to their doorstep each day, we're talking a scant few dollars more per month, much cheaper than a cable television bill, in fact.

As to restricting news alternatives in rural markets, this is a nonissue. The popularity of most community newspapers is so strong that few adjustments are needed in the first place. Also, in case it has escaped anyone's attention, we do live in an age in which the problem is more of an information glut than a vacuum.

Newspapers can cover all market segments, but they obviously cannot force anyone to read the news. All they can do is provide a good news product for those who want it, or lure the attention of marginal readers through pseudo-news and entertainment. Given the state of tight newsroom budgets, no newspaper can do both simultaneously; at least not for very long.

Proponents of the Class Appeal strategy point out that a newspaper is subsidized by advertisers who currently don't care why a consumer buys it. Maybe it is time for the newspaper itself to step up and say it does care and that it makes good business sense for the advertiser to care too. Maybe, the argument goes, it is time to start serving a news market for a change. Doing this doesn't mean the individual journalist can ignore writing creatively and engagingly, however. Even the serious news consumer is more apt to read a well-written story than a bland one.

Not all editors agree with this Class Appeal approach, however. And those who might agree still encounter trouble selling the strategy to the newspaper's publishers. One such editor, Frank Denton, has written:

What becoming more serious in further service to this quality segment might do is make us less interesting to all readers, while at the same time, the class model would have us become more expensive. That would add up to less value in a volatile and diversifying market...Do we exist to keep the educated, affluent, and/or power elite as well informed as possible? Or do we exist to inform and involve as many people as possible, to help them become more educated, affluent and powerful? Most journalists I know would choose the latter...For the most inclusive readership we need both the sizzle and the substance. That's why our jobs are so tough, and so important.[21]

It's not that journalists are deaf to reader concerns about news content. To the contrary, many think about the reader's perception of the newspaper a lot. Many of them obsess about it. They worry over what they do right and wrong in newsroom discussions, media forums, and panels. Many of these are carried out at annual meetings of journalistic organizations like SPJ, ASNE, or APME. Some of these panels are carried live by C-Span television. Some journalists, however, worry that often the emphasis is on the *mea culpa* process itself—the assumed therapeutic effect of discussion—rather than on specific responses to the problems.

Sandra Mims Rowe, former president of the Associated Press Managing Editors, said part of the ASNE credibility study addresses the widespread perception among the public that the news media are biased. In fact, she herself noted, "I have finally been persuaded that the issue of bias is probably real."[22]

Following the November 1997 summit of editors who met at the *Philadelphia Inquirer* as part of the ASNE Credibility Study, a report of the session was compiled by Arlene Notoro-Morgan, assistant managing editor at the *Inquirer.* An overview of the report, which summarizes the findings of the two-day conference, follows.

## WHAT IS CREDIBILITY?

Editors agreed that credibility is made up of the following elements: accuracy, staying connected to the readers, trust, authenticity, and behavior. Of these, accuracy looms highest in the minds of journalists. Unfortunately, the ideal of accuracy does not jibe with the practice of accuracy, which often falls short of the mark.

Some participants believed the news industry does not spend enough time assessing just how accurate the reporting is. They stressed the need to develop the measurements to test writers and put programs in place to improve the level of accuracy. Others suggested establishing an Accuracy Institute, much like the Journalism Values Institute, to study and create solutions to the ongoing accuracy problems that leave both editors and readers with the perception that journalists don't get it right often enough. Still another suggestion was to focus on how common the accuracy/tone/accessibility problems are from paper to paper and investigate if there is any correlation to why people drop their subscriptions.

Regardless of the solutions, it is important for journalists to know that accuracy is a big problem at many news organizations. Numerous research studies have shown too many errors in stories for readers in some markets to place consistent trust in their newspapers or television newscasts. One study, done by Scott Maier and published in 2002, focused on one large southern daily and found that more than half the local news stories included errors. Inaccuracies involved context and perspective, such as hype, misrepresentations, and essential information left out.[23] Maier stresses the importance of accuracy by noting:

Accuracy is the foundation of media credibility. If journalists cannot get their facts straight, how can readers trust the media to convey and interpret the news reliably? According to a national survey commissioned by the American Society of Newspaper Editors (ASNE), even small errors feed public skepticism about a newspaper's credibility. The survey also showed readers frequently notice inaccuracies in their daily newspapers.[24]

Maier surveyed 946 news sources who were identified from 553 local news stories published in the daily over a 31-day period in 1999. News sources returned 504 surveys for a response rate of slightly more than 53 percent. The per story response rate, in which at least one primary news source returned a survey, was 71 percent. The study examines errors only from the news source's perspective, and the perception of error was probably quite different from a reporter's or reader's viewpoint. Because of the nature of this particular study, the results could not be scientifically generalized to other newspapers. It simply presented a snapshot of a month's worth of stories and perceived errors in this one metro newspaper. Still, the results are interesting. For example:

- Of the 504 returned surveys, news sources identified 573 errors, or 1.1 errors per respondent.
- Some 52 percent of the respondents found at least one inaccuracy. The number of errors reported per story was 1.5.

- News sources found one or more errors in 59 percent of the 390 local news sto-ries they reviewed. Inaccuracy rates per story were slightly higher than per respondent because the majority of stories were reviewed by two news sources, thereby increasing the opportunity to catch errors.

- Sources cited factual errors more often than subjective efforts, accounting for 57 percent of the inaccuracies reported. Factual errors also tended to be substan-tive: misquotations, incorrect numbers, and inaccurate or misleading headlines were among the most commonly cited mistakes.

- Despite the introduction of electronic writing and editing technologies, the typography rate was still nearly as high as the typo rate reported in a study 60 years ago.

- The most frequently cited subjective error involved not what was reported in the newspaper but what was left out. For example, one-fourth of all subjective errors consisted of what sources considered essential information missing.

- Sources considered these subject errors more egregious than factual errors. The most severely rated inaccuracies involved contextual errors and perspective such as hype, misrepresentation, and essential information omitted.

- Least severely rated errors were those relating to location, age, and typos—errors that sources did not think affected the overall meaning of the story.

- Despite the prevalence of perceived inaccuracies, only three respondents reported requesting a correction.

- Despite the perceived inaccuracies, few sources seemed deterred from being used as future sources.

- Overall, despite these perceptions, news sources considered the newspaper in question to be a relatively credible news medium. On a seven-point scale (with 1 being the highest credibility rating), the paper received an average rat-ing of 2.6.

- Further analysis showed much more of a direct linkage between inaccuracies and story credibility rather than inaccuracies and credibility of the overall newspaper in the minds of the sources. Hence, most news sources appeared to be very forgiving of most errors, citing many of them as relatively unimportant, especially in affecting meaning of the overall story.

By several measures, the relationship between errors and newspaper credibility was statistically significant, but weak. Maier concluded that the findings suggest the public is correct in assuming there are a lot of mis-takes in newspaper copy.

However, the link between accuracy and credibility might not be as direct as presumed. While the results suggest that accuracy is an impor-tant element of story credibility, the influence of errors on any one story is not sufficient to be predictive of overall newspaper credibility. For those judgments, news sources are most concerned with how the story was played. Perhaps the industry's quest for credibility should focus less on accuracy and more on authenticity—how well each story provides balance, perspective, and context.[25]

So does this study show the industry's concern over accuracy as a credibility determinant is overblown? No, says Maier, because the industry is much more concerned about ordinary readers who are much less tolerant of errors than are the news sources cited in this study.

As to the issue of authenticity, some editors at the Philadelphia conference felt newspapers should offer more diversity in backgrounds, economics, and viewpoints of sources if they are to be believed by the general public. On behavior, Jim Naughton of the Poynter Institute of Media Studies, said the values of journalism are not the problem as much as the behavior of those who practice journalism.

An interesting comment came from John Creighton, vice president of the consulting Harwood Group, who said the reading public should be viewed as citizens; not consumers. He felt this approach should dispel the feeling in the newsrooms that industry research is too driven by market and consumer values. Thus, credibility issues must be understood in terms of their effect on the public as well as the reader. If journalists can simply remember the intonations of Thomas Jefferson and others who have argued for a free and informative press and being a prerequisite for a democracy, then the concept of marketing the news could be transformed into the concept of informing the electorate.

## HANDLING READING ANGST

Discussion among the editors in Philadelphia showed clearly that newspapers are all over the map in their approaches to self-monitoring programs like the use of ombudsmen, reader advocates, and clearing-the-record policies. Gilbert Cranbert, a professor at the University of Iowa who has been working on ombudsman studies for more than a dozen years, said the industry's overall lack of clarity in retraction/clarification policies has "significantly contributed to the public's mistrust of our profession."[26]

Suggestions for handling reader angst included the following:

- Create a "best practices" book of guidelines to show what different papers are doing to handle complaints.
- Investigate what newspapers are doing in the complaint department and find out if the public knows about these policies, has access to the paper, and generally feel that the paper handles these issues in a forthright manner.
- Examine the pattern of complains and help create solutions to the problems.
- Consider establishing an Accuracy Institute, to study and create solutions to the ongoing accuracy problems.

## COMMUNITY OUTREACH: DOES IT HELP?

Community outreach is a discussion that leads beyond the core focus of journalism as a profession of reporting, writing, and editing the news.

It leads into areas such as marketing the news, how involved journalists should be in the community or at least in caring about the community, on perceiving the community as stakeholders, and on the growing area of concern called "civic journalism" or "public journalism." Let's spend a little time on this last area.

As researcher Ann Weichelt has noted,[27] the civic journalism movement began in 1988 with the belief that the news media should take the lead in doing something about the withdrawal and disengagement of citizens. The new movement, dubbed United Beyond 2000, was led by Jack Swift, editor of the *Ledger-Enquirer* in Columbus, Georgia. The goal of the group was to get a public dialogue going with the newspaper about problems in the community. The group sponsored public forums, and Swift described the purpose as follows: "We're trying to find every way we can to help citizens empower themselves, get involved in their community, work together on mutual concerns, and make a difference."[28]

Since that time, numerous newspapers around the country have jumped into civic journalism projects including the *Wichita Eagle,* the *Charlotte Observer,* the *Star-Tribune* in Minneapolis, the *Detroit Free Press,* and the *Portland (Maine) Press Herald,* and the *Sun,* in Bremerton, Washington.

A look at just one of these projects shows what form they might take. In January 1992 the *Detroit Free Press* unveiled a Children First campaign, naming a project director and four reporters to staff the project. The publisher of the *Free Press* transferred $14,000 to the project fund, and in May the *Free Press* sponsored a day-long conference on preventing violence against children. The focus of the forum was, "Here is the problem; now how can we as a community fix it?"

Although newspapers began moving into the civic-journalism arena around the turn of the 1990s decade, local television stations had actually been working in such projects for a couple decades prior to that. For years television stations have seen the importance and value in promoting and taking host leadership roles in community projects. For example, following a series of devastating tornadoes in the late 1980s, one Indianapolis television station hosted a Twister Telethon to help raise funds for the storm victims. The same station hosted a television community forum dealing with teen suicide following several such deaths in the Indianapolis area.

In another civic-journalism project, the *Tallahassee Democrat* and WCTV-TV joined hands with financing from the Pew Charitable Trusts to conduct a survey wherein citizens reported their concerns about life in the community and what issues they felt needed change. The survey was the first activity of the Tallahassee public journalism project called Public Agenda.

And in Edmond, Oklahoma, the *Edmond Sun* hosted a public forum in the summer of 2001 to discuss the ethics of how the local media handle teenage deaths in events in which they may have been committing misdemeanor or lesser felony acts.

Not everyone in journalism embraces the notion of civic journalism, however. Several in the journalistic community feel the concept smacks of advocacy, and some fear it could be a smokescreen for a business-mandated marketing effort by the newsroom. Some feel that no matter how strongly they feel about something that's happening in the city, it is not their role to jump in with the intent of directly influencing the outcome.

Some feel that two factors have contributed to the public journalism's growth: the desire by newspaper managers to boost circulation and to win popularity for editors uncomfortable with criticism.

Nevertheless, Lewis Friedland, a professor at the University of Wisconsin who has been studying the effect of civic journalism projects for the Pew Center and Kettering Foundation, says he has found a high awareness of the civic journalism projects with readers. He reasons that the value of the projects to a newspaper's credibility is that readers are treated as partners, and as adults with a stake in what happens to the community.

And Jan Schaffer, deputy director of the Pew Center, says journalists who work with public journalism projects are more engaged and motivated. Civic journalism allows them to frame the story from the public's perspective rather than the media institution's. She also said that staff appreciate the role they now have in providing solutions to a community problem rather than simply identifying that a problem exists.[29]

Public Journalism, or Civic Journalism, can go a long way toward building bridges with readers and viewers and—therefore—added trust in the news media serving them. As previous discussion clearly indicated, credibility is a major factor with the news media these days and with the public who assess the media on a daily basis.

The ASNE thought so much of the issue it conducted a multi-year Journalism Credibility Project, begun in 1997 and funded by the Robert R. McCormick Tribune Foundation and eight daily newspapers. The lead researcher and author of the analysis was Christine D. Urban, president of Urban and Associates. The project included a representative sampling of 3,000 Americans; 16 different focus-groups; a survey sampling of 1,714 newspaper editors; a 50-member think tank of leading editors, publishers and academics; and pilot projects at eight different newspapers designed to correct credibility problems. It was a huge undertaking, and overall findings of the ASNE Credibility Project, published in August of 1999, show the following:[30]

- The public's fundamental concerns about journalism center on accuracy, the newspaper's relationship with its community, and perceptions that newspapers too often are biased and tend to overcover sensational stories.

- A thorough survey of journalists reveals areas of agreement with the public's assessment. Journalists agree with the public on the importance of accuracy—that it's more important to get a story right than to get it first.

- Most everyone—both journalists and the consumers of journalism—wants newspapers to present context and explanation, in addition to the facts.

- Journalists and the public disagree, however, on some key issues including how well local newspapers respect and understand their communities; the extent and nature of bias in news accounts, and the degree to which newspapers over-cover inherently sensational stories. Journalists' views of these factors are less troubled than the public's.

In brief, six lessons were deemed learned from the research. They are:

1. The public and the press agree there are too many factual errors and spelling or grammar mistakes in newspapers. Both put the major blame on deadline pressures. There is also great concern among the public about unnamed sources.

2. The public perceives that newspapers don't consistently demonstrate respect for, and knowledge of, their readers and communities. Journalists are much less critical of themselves. Americans feel journalists are quite willing to hurt people just to publish a story.

3. The public suspects that the points of view and biases of journalists influence what stories are covered and how they are covered. Journalists are less likely to perceive newsroom bias. Political bias, on the other hand, many not be as much of a problem for the public as journalists think it is. Americans offer journalists an element of forgiveness on the issue of bias, because they understand that every person has a different point of view. The public believes television is more biased than newspapers.

4. The public believes that newspapers overcover sensational stories because they're excited and they sell papers. Most journalists dispute the charge, and others argue they're just giving the public what they want. Additionally, most of the public thinks a story should not run if only one side can be reached for comment, but fewer than half of the journalists agree.

5. The public feels that newsroom values and practices are sometimes in conflict with their own priorities for their newspapers. Journalists seem to agree with this assessment. However, both sides agree that newspapers should hold a story until the facts can be double-checked. Additionally, the public values investigative reporting. But they feel names of suspects should be withheld until charges are filed and long-ago love trysts of public officials should be overlooked. And the public places a much higher value than do journalists on protecting the privacy of people in situations that most journalists would consider news.

6. Members of the public who have had actual experience with the news process are the most critical of media credibility. The same is true of journalists who have been the subjects of news stories themselves.

As this chapter has shown, a strong need exists to bring the reader or viewer into the equation when a journalist sits down to write. If there is a desire to really communicate and a desire to provide stories that will be read or heard, the writer must understand something about reader dynamics. Therefore, many writing coaches, editors, and journalism educators are encouraging their protégé's to consider their reader when they write. Attend any writer's conference and you will hear much advice from veteran writers who know how important it is to write to individual readers instead of a mass audience. Often this advice focuses on the following writing elements:

1. Compassion. Writers need an understanding heart and they need to be sensitive to the yearnings of their readers for more hope, more knowledge, and a better life. If writers have it, the warmth of their feeling for their readers and their concern shines through copy. If they lack it, this too can be evident and can be a sizeable barrier to understanding.[31]

2. Character. A writer should develop a style all his or her own. They should strive for a fresh, colorful, dignified and charming form of expression that represents the way they themselves talk.[32]

3. Clarity. Simplicity is the key to understanding. Good writers are precise and try to allow for only one interpretation for the thoughts they are presenting. So they seek out the right word for the right job. They also emphasize the short word. Author Gelett Burgess says short words are strong words and work well. Illustrating this, he writes:

When we are tired sore, when we faint with fear, or pain stings...Or when we blaze with wrath, then we cry out: "Help me! Come quick!" We snarl, "You lie, you cur!" We wail, "Oh woe is me!" Or moan, "She is gone. She has left me. She does not love me!" Bad words are all short, too. They bite. They are vile. They say what they mean. For short words come from deep down in our hearts; not from our brains. They are like the bones of speech that make talk firm and hard. Like blood that gives life. Long words are the fat and thews and skin that make speech fair of form. But with a lack of short words, what one says has less truth and zest. Less youth, too.[33]

4. Suspense. The essence of thinking like a writer is recognizing that what the reader finds most interesting is the unknown; not the known. So thinking like a writer prizes the question more than the answer, and it celebrates paradox, mystery, and uncertainty, recognizing that all of them contain the seeds of a potential story. Curiosity sends writers on the quests, and curiosity is what makes readers read the stories that result.[34]

And finally, consider the following advice from some of the world's best writers:[35]

- "Make 'em laugh; make 'em cry...make 'em wait."—Ring Lardner.
- "Agatha Christie has given more pleasure in bed than any other woman."—Nancy Banks-Smith.
- "A good writer is basically a storyteller; not a scholar or a redeemer of mankind."—Isaac Basshevis Singer.
- "The power to determine each day what shall be important and what shall be neglected is power unlike any that has been exercised since the Pope lost his hold on the secular mind."—Walter Lippmann.

Clearly, some of the best writers are those who enjoy telling stories and engaging the minds and imaginations of readers or viewers with their carefully styled writing.

## NOTES

1. Lauren Kessler and Duncan McDonald, *When Words Collide* (Belmont, Calif.: Wadsworth, 1984), 5.
2. G. Stuart Adam, *The Poynter Papers: No. 2. Notes Toward a Definition of Journalism: Understanding an Old Craft as an Art Form* (St. Petersburg, Fla.: Poynter Institute, 1993), 11.
3. Ibid., 15.
4. Ibid., 14.
5. Ibid., 16.
6. Jim Willis, "Farewell: Emotions Run High at Murrah Building Ceremony," *Edmond (Okla.) Evening Sun,* 17 May 1995, 1.
7. *Harper's Book of Quotations* (New York: HarperCollins, 1992), 494.
8. Walt Harrington, *Intimate Journalism: The Art and Craft of Reporting Everyday Life* (Thousand Oaks, Calif.: Sage, 1997), 108.
9. Jack Hart, "Writing to Be Read," *Editor & Publisher* (12 April 1993): 5.
10. Jim Willis, "Editors, Readers and News Judgment," *Editor & Publisher* (7 Feb 1987) 32.
11. Robert Leon Baker, "Romancing Your Readers," *Impact: A Newsletter on Trends, Techniques and Tools for Communicators* (Chicago, 1980): 1.
12. Ibid., 2.
13. Ibid., 1.
14. John McManus, "Serving the Public and Serving the Market: A Conflict of Interest?" *Journal of Mass Media Ethics,* 7, no. 4 (1992): 198–199.
15. Ibid., 197ff.
16. Ibid., 199.
17. Jim Willis, "Editors, Readers and News Judgment," *Editor & Publisher* (7 February 1987): 14–15.
18. Joseph P. Bernt et al., "How Well Can Editors Predict Reader Interest in News?" *Newspaper Research Journal,* 21, no. 2 (Spring 2000): 2–9.

19. Ibid., 8–9.

20. Jim Willis, "Class Appeal vs. Mass Appeal," *The American Editor* (March 1998): 8–9.

21. Frank Denton, "Reaction: Market for Readers Isn't That Simple," *The American Editor* (March 1998): 9.

22. Sandra Mims Rowe, in a talk at the *Philadelphia Inquirer,* Philadelphia, Pa., 7 November 1997.

23. Scott Maier, "Getting It Right? Not in 59 Percent of Stories," *Newspaper Research Journal,* 23, no. 1 (Winter 2002): 10–22.

24. Ibid.

25. Ibid.

26. Statements made at the *Philadelphia Inquirer* in a meeting of editors, 5 November 1997.

27. Ann Weichelt, "Public Journalism: Leadership or Readership?" (Paper presented to the Association for Education in Journalism and Mass Communication, Washington, August 1995).

28. Ibid.

29. Ibid.

30. Christine Urban, ed., *Examining Our Credibility: Perspectives of the Public and the Press* (Reston, Va.: American Society of Newspaper Editors, 1999). Also available online at www.asne.org.

31. Robert Leon Baker, "The Seven C's of the Writing Art," *Impact: A Newsletter on Trends, Techniques and Tools for Communicators* (Chicago, 1980): 1.

32. Ibid.

33. Ibid., 2.

34. James Stewart, in a speech at the Poynter National Writers Workshop, Portland, Ore., organized by the Poynter Institute of Media Studies, St. Petersburg, Fla., April 1999. Also available online at www.poynter.org.

35. *Harper's Book of Quotations.* (New York: HarperCollins, 1992), 492, 502, 503.

# Chapter 7

# Journalists and Emotions: From Oklahoma City and Beyond

This is the first of two discussions dealing with journalists and the personal emotions they encounter when covering stories. It seems to be a natural continuation of the discussion on writing that the previous chapter analyzed.

A long-held tradition of news reporting dictates that journalists should somehow separate themselves from their emotions while on the job and should detach—if not distance themselves entirely—from the people, issues, and events they are covering. This is seen by many as the essence of objectivity, and objectivity has long been a cornerstone of the journalistic profession.

In the afterword prepared by Dr. Ann Norwood, a psychiatrist with the U.S. Army, we will look at some of the emotional impact on journalists and on the public of the traumatic events that journalists cover. In this chapter we will look at this issue of reporter detachment from the stories he or she covers, how difficult that is to accomplish at times, and whether it really does get one closer to the truth or, perhaps, doesn't.

As chapter 2 discussed, reporters approach their stories from a variety of perspectives. Some of these are more rationally or cognitively oriented; some are more emotionally or affectively oriented. If a journalist were to look for a patron saint of ethics to guide him or her in the quest for the appropriate cognitive or effective approach to his or her craft, he or she could do worse than to study the Greek philosopher Aristotle, who opened his own school of logic, the Lyceum, in 334 B.C. Greece of those days could be compared, at least to some extent, to America today. Democracy was a cherished ideal to all citizens of that country. Family values were an important part of the country's make-up. Cultural diversity was the norm, and thinkers—great and small—were generally free to discuss the great mysteries of life in the art of philosophy.

Aristotle believed that the purpose of ethics in human life was to help make people happy, and that the only way to do this was through a set of intangible laws, called ethics. Through these laws could a person become truly happy and truly good. To reach those goals, a person must find a middle point between virtue and vice in life, and between reason and passion.[1] To Aristotle, attaining happiness and conforming to ethics was a matter of having a purpose in life. In that purpose, there must be truth. Aristotle was always searching for truth, and it was his belief that if truth could not be established in a search, then there was little value in that search or that endeavor.

In Aristotle's day, most philosophers focused on what life would be like in an ideal world; not the real world. They tried to convince people that an ideal life would benefit them and all humankind. But Aristotle saw folly in these ideas. To him, there was no ideal world. No matter how hard humans try, there would always be more ideals toward which we would strive. So he counseled what he called "practical wisdom" for the real world. He was a believer in common sense and once said that "any view that flies in the face of common sense simply could not be true." He counseled his students to consider the good not only in their conclusions, but also in their premises. In other words, consider why you do what you do before you do it. What is the reason or purpose for your action in a certain situation? Is it for personal satisfaction, glorification, revenge maybe? To him, there are unethical motives for action.

Aristotle also believed reason is our greatest gift as humans, and he focused a lot of his attention on studying the ethics upon the way people reason. He counseled, when confronted with any ethical dilemma, rely on your ability to reason it out. But he also counseled students to search for moral virtue in all their causes. Again, he believed we should find a golden mean between reason and passion in everyday life. Whenever confronted with a dilemma and a quick mean must be found, he advised, always lean toward the virtuous side. And the life that exhibits the virtues is summed up most generally by Aristotle as life according to reason.

Notwithstanding his love of reason, Aristotle also counseled students to listen to their passions and emotions. Intuition and feelings should be your allies, he would say. These feelings, sometimes called inner judgments or intuition, are an important guiding force. They are run by our conscience, which sets us apart from other animals. And while generally aligning reason with virtue and passions with vice, he said time and again that we shouldn't ignore either in our actions. Reason, he advised, does not exclude passion, because passions are an inexpungible part of the human psyche.[2] The only question is how one incorporates these passions—these emotions—into the everyday human life. These passions are indeed emotional feelings that are generally accompanied by pleasure or pain. They are feelings like anger, fear, hope, loyalty, admiration, love, joy, and hatred. They often constitute the motivation for actions among human beings, and they are precisely the field of operations for the moral virtues. A moral virtue is a state of character on the basis of which we act and stand well with reference to the passions.

The measure of rightness of our actions or moral virtue? To Aristotle that measure was incorporating passions into our lives under the guiding light of reason. Again, it is a search for that golden mean, which may be different for each of us at different times and for different decisions we face in our lives.

I like Aristotle as a guiding voice in deciding what a reporter should do with the emotions he or she encounters in covering a story in which people are in the grip of strong passions. I believe there must be a blending of emotion and reason guiding journalists in their reporting and writing, more so for some kinds of stories than others. The following discussion should help define what I mean.

It seems appropriate here to share some personal observations accumulated after years of reflecting on some stories I've covered in my own reporting career. These are cases in which I know a journalist's emotions have affected him personally and his stories. I will interweave these personal observations with insights from other writers about their own work.

Years ago I was showing a new reporter the ropes in Dallas. He was a different kind of recruit for us at the newspaper. He was a Dallas Cowboy football star who had been a first-round draft pick out of the University of Wyoming at the cornerback position. Unlike many of his teammates, this man was already thinking beyond football, however, and wanted to get experience in his chosen major of journalism. He was a bright guy, and as editor of the paper I welcomed the chance to mentor him. The paper had hired him as a summer intern and I was taking him around to a couple coverage sites to show him reporting, up close and personal.

This particular day, we were at the site of a car-train collision, and the mangled body of the driver was still behind the wheel of the twisted auto wreckage. I had seen this before, back in Oklahoma, covering a similar car-train wreck. But for Aaron, the sight of violent death was brand new and, despite the blood he had seen over the years on the gridiron, this was much different and a bit too much for him at the moment. He excused himself for a moment and strode over to a nearby tree to compose himself. I thought it was a scene similar to what a new medical student must feel the first time he or she sees blood—or perhaps death—in the operating room.

I understood what he was feeling, and I wasn't concerned as much by his reaction as by my own. While he was feeling what any normal person would feel at seeing such a gruesome sight, I was the one with the abnormal reaction because I wasn't feeling much of anything. I wondered: Have I been in this business too long? Am I becoming so hardened that I can't experience a normal rush of emotional grief over witnessing such a tragedy? Or have I just become so good at burying those feelings so I can go about my daily routine of distancing myself from life so I can report on it accurately? And if that is what I'm doing, then isn't there a paradox built into that logic? Can I really report accurately on a life that I am distancing myself from? And even if I could, wouldn't the reader sense that I just don't care about what I'm witnessing?

The gifted writer George Orwell once noted that the great enemy of clear writing is insincerity. Those who believe this question whether readers or viewers will be engaged by a piece if they don't feel the writer cares about the story. It is not that he or she has an opinion about the issue involved or who might be to blame—just that he or she cares about the people involved in the story. If writers do care, then their writing should show it. I have come to believe that myself. I have asked myself if we as reporters are not trying too much for a sense of neutral sterility in our reporting, and if the reader can find any warmth or empathy at all in that kind of writing.

Others I know in this business have spoken often of the way they were personally moved by stories they covered, so I know I'm not alone in my thinking—or rather feeling. Take for example Mary Walsh, a highly gifted senior producer for CBS News. Recently Mary wrote me about a story she had covered years ago in China about a stalwart ballet company determined to succeed despite laboring under the worst conditions and with few financial resources. Their costumes were what most Westerners would consider rags, but that didn't deter them from pursuing excellence in their art. Mary wrote that it was an extremely moving experience for her personally, and I'm sure that sense of emotional engagement made her piece even more moving.

Another experience stands out in my memory. Springtime 1995 I was home visiting my parents in Oklahoma City on spring break from my teaching post at Boston College. Wednesday morning, April 19, I was eating breakfast in a diner called Jimmy's Egg, in Norman about 20 minutes south of downtown Oklahoma City. In the midst of breakfast I heard a strange, muffled sound coming from somewhere in the distance. A few minutes later, the television in the back of the diner bulletined the news and defined that sound. The Alfred P. Murrah Federal Building had just been attacked. There was an explosion. Some people could be dead. Before I knew it, I was a reporter once again, covering the aftermath for an Oklahoma daily, The *Edmond Evening Sun,* which I had edited years before. The *Sun* serves an upscale Oklahoma City suburb that lost 20 residents in the Murrah Building bombing.

For the next two months I was living and breathing the greatest catastrophe this state has ever known. Until the World Trade Center bombing on September 11, 2001, it would be America's worst case of terrorism on its own soil. I took a leave from Boston College and produced more than 50 stories related to the bombing and its aftermath. Unlike the times back in Dallas when I found myself numb at the site of violent death, however, this time was different. I felt more at ease with myself because this time I found myself feeling a great amount of sadness every time I showed up at the bombing site to do my day's reporting. For one thing, this is the city where I grew up. I used to swim with the Boy Scouts in the Downtown Y located just across Fifth Street from the Murrah carnage. That Y was now a darkened, hollowed-out shell of a building. There was a feeling I could not shake that this was my city, and the people I know had been grimly attacked.

Try as I might, I could not distance myself from these emotions. And, in this failure, I found myself wondering if those emotions would not warp or distort my reporting. As I would soon discover—perhaps not so surprisingly—the exact opposite occurred. It was my sadness that helped me understand and relate better to the people I interviewed and who were caught up in sadness themselves. One such person was Miami fireman Skip Fernandez, who I found sitting in full battle gear on a curb at Sixth and Robinson with the look of utter exhaustion pouring from his body. It was my first morning at Ground Zero, and Skip was accompanied on the curb by his Golden Retriever Aspen, one of the many search-and-rescue dogs used to locate bodies. They were leaning on each other, and Aspen carried a look of sadness I've seldom seen on any face, animal or human. It was about 9 a.m. and they had just come off their 10-hour stint on the rubble pile looking for bodies and body parts. They were spent, but Skip wanted to talk about what he had seen and what he was feeling.

Since reporters were not allowed on the rubble pile—and in fact were kept a block away from the bomb site itself—Skip had seen things up close that I could only imagine. I wanted to know what he knew; I wanted to see what he saw; I wanted to feel what he felt. Not just for morbid curiosity, but for accuracy itself. As were so many other stories in the aftermath of the bombing, this story was essentially about emotions. How could I write accurately unless I could feel accurately what he felt?

But there was another reason for my curiosity: I found myself caring deeply about this tragedy and about Skip and all the other searchers who were asked to do and see what he had done and seen. And I didn't mind that feeling one bit. After checking internally and asking the inevitable questions reporters ask ("Is that wrong?" "Aren't I supposed to be detached?"), I realized again these stories are largely about emotions and that to ignore those emotions would be to miss the story entirely. The actual body count, be it 150 or 200, is important but there are other things equally as important. This is a tragedy of massive proportions, and that is important. And this event has made a whole lot of people very sad and has thrust them into grieving from which they must somehow recover. And that is important. And through it all, these people are responding magnificently. And that is important.

And fueling all of this are people's emotions. The survivors, the families, the friends, the rescuers, the volunteers. Even the reporters. I will never forget something I saw a couple weeks later at an improvised memorial service held right on the rubble pile. A Reuters cameraman had dangled a beautiful red, dewy rose from his tripod in his own personal memory of those who had perished in the attack. So I felt that to deny or turn the focus away from emotions—to distance myself too much from all of this—came closer to distorting the reality of it than did allowing myself to feel and to bring all those senses into my stories.

I know there are many who feel this is too maudlin for reporters to get attached to stories and the people they cover. I know that, in a strange way, familiarity breeds contempt and that we have all been overexposed to a multitude of emotions emanating from the Oklahoma City bombing and even more so from the World Trade Center attacks. I know words like "Heartland," "Ground Zero," "Grief," "Closure," and "Hero" have been used so much that they've lost their resonance to many people. I know that, in their search for larger audiences, some media are prone toward sensationalizing and hyping stories beyond their factual drama. I am aware of the slow-motion scenes of weary firemen floating by and the pro-longed shots of tears from victims' families. I am aware of reporters' efforts to go for the reader's or viewer's emotional jugular. I am not a fan of hyped emotions; of overlaying theatrical emotions on the real emotions of the moment. I do, however, distinguish between factual and hyped emotions. I see no problem reporting the former because they are as much of the reporting scene as the who, the what, or the why. The latter are noth-ing but exploitation for market gain, and I detest them.

Through it all, it seems that if a reporter is going to write a story that is essentially about emotions, he or she should not fear experiencing those emotions themselves. As I discovered in the Oklahoma City experience, such emotional attachment can even have profound effects on the reporter himself. On the three-year anniversary of the Murrah Building bombing I was asked by the *Edmond Evening Sun* to write about what the experience of covering the tragedy had meant for me. This is what I wrote:

I told myself I came back to visit my family, but I could have picked any weekend for that. For months in the back of my mind was this one weekend, especially Sunday, April 19. Coming back to the bomb site three years later. Coming back to a pivotal point in my life. Coming back to remember...and hopefully to feel again.

Three years ago I had been visiting my parents in Oklahoma City, on leave from my teaching post at Boston College and trying to put the wheels back on my life's Radio Flyer. A shattering personal experience had left that wagon in pieces, scattered across a thousand miles of grieving.

I was searching for a way to forget. Or at least to deal with the pain. Then on Wednesday morning, April 19, 1995, my personal pain collided with a far greater collective pain that emerged from the cloud of dust, debris and devastation that was the bombing of the Alfred P. Murrah Federal Building.

Hearing a distant, undefinable rumble from a diner in Norman, I didn't realize at first how this event would affect me personally. By the end of the day, however, that reality was streaming in like a door to a dark room; opening slowly, gradually allowing the outside light to seep in and flood the room.

I have been in the news business for three decades and have seen a hundred faces of tragedy during that time. There was the sweet innocence of a 5-year-old girl who was killed by a falling beam as she sat in church one Sunday morning in Garland, Texas, 20 years ago. Ten years ago in Boston, Charles Stuart turned a gun on his pregnant wife moments after emerging from a class on childbirth. Blaming it first on a black attacker, Stuart later took his own life after the police realized he himself had been the shooter.

Then, just a few weeks ago, there was the tragedy of the four children and their teacher gunned down in a Jonesboro, Ark., middle school. In between there have been so many other stories of pain that they have faded into a collective blur over the years.

All except the Oklahoma City bombing.

As a journalist who now teaches future reporters and editors, I have trained myself to put distance between me and the pain of others. I have coached my students to do the same. Remember what you are, I say. Do your job first. Remain objective and detached. Yes, there are times when the pain invades you personally. But those are usually in the quiet, reflective moments after the tragedy—if in fact there is time for such moments.

Always, though, there are the exceptions to the rule.

Thankfully, for me, Oklahoma City was that exception in the spring of 1995. It may sound macabre to say I found a renewed energy and life force in such a tragedy. But I did. I needed a way to express my own pain, and I found it in joining with others who were grieving over something much more painful. What a privilege it was to have the chance to articulate their pain. What a catharsis it was to be able to release my own in the process.

Over the three years since the bombing, I have spoken to many groups, both in the United States and Europe, about covering this tragedy. Always the thought is with me that I grew personally and moved beyond my personal grief as I watched survivors and families of the victims do the same. In telling their story of survival, I was also telling my own. To myself, anyway.

On a professional level, I had been confronting burnout with this business of journalism going into April, 19, 1995. I wondered if there was any real reason for journalists to go running around, exposing the pain, problems and perils of others. By the end of my first day of bombing coverage, I had found a new meaning in this profession. I am sure the same has happened to reporters covering such tragedies as the assassinations of John F. Kennedy and Martin Luther King.

Such journalism puts all humanity on the same page in the hymnal of brother-hood, understanding and support. Such journalism is washed clean of the manip-ulation and sensationalism of pseudo-news and trash reporting. Such journalism deals openly with the gut questions that friends and families of the dead and suf-fering are desperately seeking answers to. Questions like what happened and why did it happen? What can we learn from it?

Most of these questions lie beyond the boundaries of daily journalism. The answers—or at least some clues—are found in conversations with friends and loved ones, or in reading books written by those authors gifted at thoughtful reflection, or in spiritual counseling.

But journalism can help. It can act as a lighthouse or a search beacon, pointing to those issues that need to be considered and discussed. It can open the doors to the mind and heart as it shows all of us we are not alone in our grief and that there are others who can help us.

And it can make even the most objective of us feel the emotions that make us real people.

Sunday night, with all ten fingers laced through the chain-link fence separating the mourners from the insanity of that bombing, with my eyes fixed on the hal-lowed ground before me and with the vivid memory of what that killing ground looked like three years ago, the feelings did return. I knew that, in feeling for oth-ers and helping to articulate their grief, I had become whole again.[3]

Ironically, a year after writing this retrospective, I was thrust into the path of another story that would pose yet another test for what I, as a jour-nalist, should do with my emotions.

Once again I was visiting my parents in Oklahoma, attending an event at my old high school in Midwest City, a suburb of Oklahoma City. On the night of the ceremony, I was at the school with my parents and sister. The skies outside had been ominous. There was a wild tornado dancing around in Chickasha, a town 40 miles to the southwest. But we expected only rain and that patented Oklahoma lightning. The dinner was just underway when the principal arose, went to the lectern, and announced calmly that the twister that had been in Chickasha an hour before was now on the out-skirts of Midwest City. Perhaps it was time for us to adjourn the dinner and move into the basement locker rooms of the field house.

Most of the hundred gathered readily obeyed. Growing up in Okla-homa, this is a routine you encounter a lot in the spring and summer. Tor-nado Alley, the state is called. Most threats produce little damage, but this time things looked bad. We filed out under the covered walkway across the parking lot to the J. E. Sutton Field House. It was raining hard now, and tennis-ball-size hailstones were clanging off the aluminum walkway roof. In the subterranean locker rooms, below the basketball court, many of us huddled around a television and saw a surreal sight: A huge twister, deter-mined to be a monstrous F-5, is chewing up real estate in Moore, just south of the Midwest City border. As the television eye in the sky shows clearly, it is coming our way. There's our unmistakable black-and-gold water tower in the distance, and we are huddled just a couple blocks from it in the locker room. It is a collision-course scenario as the funnel weaves and bobs northward, taking out power stations, homes, businesses and everything else in its path. There are explosions and sparks flying into the night skies as transformers blow.

At that moment, we are thrust into blackness as the school's power supplies succumb to the high winds and lightning outside. Only a portable radio from the floor alerts us that we are in imminent danger. Then, as often happens with these storms, the half-mile-wide funnel veers left at the last minute and heads north up Air Depot Boulevard, about four blocks west of us. On its way, it takes about more than 200 homes and five lives.

After the all-clear sounded at the high school, I found myself in my car trying to find a clear road out of the debris that now defines much of the west side of Midwest City. This is an experience I desperately wanted to write about, and I was headed to the newsroom of *The Daily Oklahoman* in neighboring Oklahoma City. My journalistic friends greet me there, but Managing Editor Ed Kelley jokingly asks if I can't make my trips to Oklahoma a little less frequent, as recently I have brought disaster along with me. First the Murrah Building bombing, now this storm. For now, though, he wants my story, and it is now he who wants to feel what I have just felt huddling in that locker room.

So I am at a work station once again, pounding out a story and—once again—emotion is fueling my writing. In some ways it is like the adrenaline an athlete feels going into a game. You're trying to stay composed enough to do a professional job on the field, but you also want the emotions to propel you to an even greater height of performance.

I remember what novelist Joan Didion said once when she wrote, "I write entirely to find out what I'm feeling." And what writer E. M. Forster said when he noted, "How can I know what I think until I see what I say?" And Henry David Thoreau as he asked, "How vain it is to sit down to write when you have not stood up to live."[4] The events of this evening and the past few years had brought me to a clearer understanding of all these insights. Writing to find out what I feel...it happened in the spring of 1995, and four years later it is happening again on this spring night.

I slip into the narrative without knowing it. I am reliving the night. I am reliving it for the readers who weren't in the twister's path but who know others who were. But I am also reliving it for me. I am writing to find out what I feel. It seems to work, and the story is writing itself and is done within the hour. What emerged was a story about a few hundred people waiting to be hit by the tornado of the century, wondering what it would be like, and ultimately dodging the bullet at the last minute.

Often the traditional journalistic community is more tolerant with the idea of weaving emotions into a story about an event the reporter has experienced firsthand. In such a case, the reporter becomes a witness to history and fills the dual role of reporter and source. To deny such a voice to a person who is trained in written expression seems foolish indeed. Think, for example, how much a writer like the *New York Times'* Katherine E. Finkelstein can bring to an event like the World Trade Center attacks—an event she experienced firsthand. In an *American Journalism Review* essay, she writes about what that experience was like. In part, "40 Hours in Hell" reads:

I fought against the tide of employees, past one rescue command center and down to the entrance of the north tower, where the dust and paper storm felt thicker. I was feet from the door through which employees were being evacuated. The sunlight was gone, the air thick with ash. People waiting to leave were backed up the stairwell in what looked like an endless line.

It is hard now to say what I heard or saw first. A low and ominous rumble, in a split second turning into a roar. A vast black cloud forming at the top of the south tower, then sinking quickly as though the building were made of fabric, not steel. The orderly effort to evacuate people splintering as people broke from the door and raced past me. A man shouted into a walkie-talkie. People yelled out, "It's going to go!" As the building collapsed, black funnels of debris raced toward us, about to overtake us. I turned east and barreled up a side street, the lethal column of debris at my back.

  This cannot be real, I thought for a nanosecond, arms pumping, legs flying. I am running for my life up a street I have known all my life, being chased by a building. It's like a demented Bruce Willis movie.

  "Let's go, let's go," an FBI man screamed from the mouth of a subway entrance. Two cops hurtled in. I leapt in after them and almost fell down the stairs as the pulverized building thundered over me.

  I am being buried alive, I thought.[5]

How can you tell a reporter to leave emotions out of a story like that? Even if they weren't underneath the falling rubble but showed up hours later and saw the devastation, the blood, smelled the charred bodies, and saw and heard the anguish of others who had been there, is there that much difference in letting them include the emotional impact that any normal witness would feel? As long as it is an accurate description, what harm is there in allowing it? Doesn't such a description actually come closer to capturing the truth and transporting the reader to the scene of the tragedy?

Concerning television coverage of the Twin Towers attacks, some journalists have critiqued the emotions they saw evinced in some of the top anchors for the networks ABC, CBS, and NBC. Writer Lori Robertson noted that ABC's Peter Jennings had difficulty even getting the words of the September 11 attack out of his mouth on that fateful Monday. "He swallowed a few times," she notes, "blinked a lot, (and) avoided eye contact with the camera."[6] Jennings had trouble with coherency once or twice and injected his own urging to parents when he said on-air:

We do not very often make recommendations for people's behavior from this chair, but as (ABC News correspondent) Lisa (Stark) was talking, I checked in with my children and it—who were deeply stressed, as I think young people are across the United States. So, if you're a parent, you've got a kid...in some other part of the country, call them up. Exchange observations.[7]

Even stoic Dan Rather broke down and cried during an appearance on *The Late Show with David Letterman,* after the September 11 attacks. However, both Rather and Jennings believe it is important for news anchors to stay calm and show no emotions while on the air reporting the news. Says Jennings, "It's not my role to impose my emotional state on the audience."[8] About his urging to parents on September 11, he continued, "And even now as I tell you about it, I have an emotional reaction, which I didn't anticipate at the time. Those kinds of things you cannot help, but I think you have to be very, very careful...People are so on edge that you don't want to contribute to them going over the edge one way or another on a given subject."[9]

Rather agreed and said, "This (the World Trade Center attacks) is a unique situation. I've never had as much difficulty as I did in this...I'm not robotized; I'm not hypnotized. I try very hard not to let my emotions show. Sometimes it's unavoidable."[10]

Robert J. Thompson, who teaches media and popular culture at Syracuse University, isn't sure that such emotional displays by newspeople is so bad, especially in such settings as Rather's appearance on the Letterman show. "I think his (Rather's) stock went way up. The incident established a level of concern and humility."[11] This comment seems to echo the belief many have that readers and viewers become more engaged in a story if they feel the reporter cares about the story, the people in it, and cares enough about the reader or viewer to write a story evidencing that care. However, Thompson adds, weeping in the anchor chair is probably not a good thing. "I think that would have been a totally different situation. That would have been very alarming."[12]

Robertson quotes longtime CBS anchor Walter Cronkite as saying, "I would worry about an individual who did not show some emotion at a time like this. I think obviously it should not be so excessive that it interferes with doing the job."[13]

Does showing support for those killed and injured in a tragedy cross the line for reporter objectivity? Does wearing a tricolor ribbon of the kind passed around after the Oklahoma City bombing or the World Trade Center attacks violate reporter objectivity? Does urging support and unity for the United States cross the line? These are all issues that have been debated in the journalistic community after these and other tragedies. Some believe journalists should wear no ribbons or other visible emblems like American flag pins that might give an appearance of taking sides or bias. Others feel these emblems are simply signs of support and respect for those impacted and should not be confused with showing support of a particular government policy or position. In the aftermath of the World Trade Center attacks, some television networks issued mandates for their on-air talent to doff the ribbons or pins. Meanwhile, many local station affiliates left the decision up to their individual staff members, and many news anchors and reporters chose to wear the emblems of support.

I'd like to intersperse here some observations from psychologist Daniel Goleman, author of a 1995 book called, *Emotional Intelligence.* Goleman has uncommonly good insight into things affecting journalists. He was once interviewed extensively by Bill Moyers for an episode of a PBS series called *The Public Mind.* This particular episode was called, "The Truth About Lies." It dealt with the epidemic of lying in America, and Goleman had just written an important book called *Vital Lies, Simple Truths.* In *Emotional Intelligence,* Goleman begins with a quote I like from Antoine De Saint-Exupery's *The Little Prince:* "It is with the heart that one sees rightly; what is essential is invisible to the eye."

As Goleman talks about our two minds, the rational and emotional, he notes:

The emotional/rational dichotomy approximates the folk distinction between "heart" and "head;" knowing something is right "in your heart" is a different order of conviction—somehow a deeper kind of certainty—than thinking so with your rational mind... These two minds, the emotional and the rational, operate in tight harmony for the most part...

Feelings are essential to thought, thought to feeling. But when passions surge, the balance tips; it is the emotional mind that captures the upper hand, swamping the rational mind.[14]

It is the last paragraph in this quote that I feel is so important for journalists to understand. In times of increased passion, emotions play a larger part in our thought processes. And perhaps this is not such a bad thing. Emotional events might well call for an appropriate emotional expression to convey them accurately to the audience. And, unless the reporter is superhuman, he or she may not even have a choice in the matter. According to Goleman, they will be emotional, to one degree or another, in this setting.

In conclusion, perhaps we shouldn't see emotions as such frivolous or negative things when it comes to reporting or the decisions reporters make when they do that reporting. Clearly it is the adrenaline factor that often gets an enterprising reporter past high hurdles and to the finish line that journalists call the deadline. Goleman points out the role that emotions play in our actions. Two examples, out of many, suffice to explain his concept:[15]

- With fear, blood goes to the large skeletal muscles, such as the legs, making it easier to flee. At the same time, the body freezes, if only for a moment, perhaps allowing time to gauge whether hiding might be a better reaction. Circuits in the brain's emotional centers trigger a flood of hormones that put the body on general alert, making it edgy and ready for action. And attention fixates on the threat at hand, the better to evaluate what response to make.

- An essential role of sadness is to help us adjust to a great loss. Sadness brings a reduction in energy and enthusiasm for life's activities, particularly diversions and pleasures, and—as it deepens and approaches depression—slows the body's metabolism. This introspective withdrawal creates the opportunity to mourn a loss or frustrated hope, grasp its consequences for one's life. As energy returns, it lets us plan new beginnings. This loss of energy may well have kept saddened—and vulnerable—early humans close to home, where they were safer.

Perhaps it is not so important for us to try to divorce ourselves from our emotions as to try to follow the advice of Socrates who advised his students, "Know thyself." If we can come to know and recognize our emotions and channel them into producing accurate and engaging stories, what is wrong with that?

Jon Franklin, writer of "Mrs. Kelly's Monster" that won a Pulitzer Prize, once recalled John Steinbeck talking about holding fire in his hands. Then as was composing Mrs. Kelly's Monster, Franklin says, "I never knew what that meant. I started reading it through and I noticed that my heart was racing. The piece was having a physiological effect on me. Whatever the hell it was, it was a moment you do not forget when you get a feeling from your own piece. God it was fun."[16]

I have been fortunate in feeling that twice now, I realized that evening in Oklahoma City. Both times it happened in Oklahoma City, and both times it was because I allowed myself to report on factual emotions. Missing these emotions would have been as egregious to the accuracy of the story as misrepresenting the events or people or making up things that people did not say. Factual emotions are simply woven into the fabric of the story and should not be missed.

The best journalism today is done by reporters who are willing to take risks. Risks in their reporting, but also risks in their writing. Neither gives you an immediate sense of comfort. Such feelings of stage fright are nothing new with writers.

Then there are those memories shared by writer Sebastian Junger in the afterword of his best-selling, *The Perfect Storm*. Junger reminisces about his experiences reporting this tragedy wherein six commercial fishermen lost their lives at sea. Junger became emotionally attached to the story and found himself caring deeply about the crew and their loved ones.

As writers perhaps we should try to put ourselves in the place and mindset of those people we cover so we can understand how they must feel and why they react as they do. And I agree with Franklin, Didion, and Millay that we should let ourselves experience the thrill of such reporting risks at least once in awhile. I'm convinced our readers and viewers—as well as the people we write about—will benefit greatly from the experience.

## NOTES

1. Paul Crittenden, *Learning to Be Moral: Philosophical Thoughts About Moral Development* (London: Humanities Press, 1990), 103–110.

2. Ibid.

3. Jim Willis, "Journalists Heal Wounds During Bombing," *Edmond (Okla.) Evening Sun*, 19 April 1998, 5.

4. Robert I. Fitzhenry, ed., *The Harper book of Quotations*, 3rd. ed. (New York: HarperCollins, 1993), 491–495.

5. Katherine E. Finkelstein, "40 Hours in Hell," *American Journalism Review* (November 2001): 30–31.

6. Lori Robertson, "Anchoring the Nation," *American Journalism Review* (November 2001): 45.

7. Ibid., 40–41.

8. Ibid., 41–42.

9. Ibid.

10. Ibid.

11. Ibid.

12. Ibid.

13. Ibid.

14. Daniel Goleman, *Emotional Intelligence*, (New York: Bantam Books, 1995), 3–9.

15. Ibid.

16. Jon Franklin as quoted in Walt Harrington, *Intimate Journalism* (Thousand Oaks, Calif.: Sage, 1995), 108.

# Afterword: Journalists and Traumatic Stress

*By Col. Ann Norwood, M.D., Associate Professor of Psychiatry, Uniformed Services University of Health and Sciences, Mary Walsh, senior producer, **CBS News**, and Penny Owen, reporter, **The Daily Oklahoman**.*

It was an item on the evening news like so many others from Somalia in December 1992—an emaciated infant was dying of starvation. Only in this case, the baby girl died as the camera rolled. As life passed from her tiny body, the picture began to shake ever so slightly. The cameraman had begun to cry; he wept silently as he continued shooting the video—one more emotional wound for *CBS News* cameraman Kurt Hoeffle who has covered war, genocide, and calamity for 30 years.

"You cry while you're covering it," Hoeffle says of stories like the famine that killed thousands of Somalis. "You see things that are terrible to watch." In 1994, Hoeffle covered a human disaster of epic proportions in Goma, Zaire. A cholera epidemic hit hundreds of thousands of refugees as they fled a genocidal war in neighboring Rwanda. "They were trying to make it to the camp (in Goma). It was only two kilometers up the road, but you could see they didn't have the strength. They were dying on the street right there in front of you." Journalists covering the catastrophe slept in tents on the edge of the refugee camp and awoke each morning to count the dead just outside their shelters. "That was the worst scene," said Hoeffle. "On a good day, there were 20 bodies. On a bad day, it was 200."[1]

To date, there have been only a handful of studies of how journalists react to the violence, chaos, and sorrow they encounter on the job, none of them definitive. There is anecdotal evidence that reporters like other professionals who are exposed to trauma—firefighters, police, combat veterans—suffer emotional aftershocks and are at risk for psychiatric consequences of traumatic exposure.

*Newsweek* correspondent Donatella Lorch spent 3 years in Africa, much of it reporting from war zones. She wrote of her experiences in the *Media Studies Journal,* describing her own emotional distress that continued even when she had returned home to the United States. "I struggled with an emptiness that I nursed alone at night…deeply lonely, anxious and unhappy. I lived with insomnia and jumbled nightmares that even today occasionally intrude."[2]

Are journalists at risk for the psychiatric consequences of trauma that they witness? Lorch's article in *Media Studies* offers anecdotal evidence that they are. Of journalists she has known, Lorch wrote, "I have watched many drink heavily and at least one slip into alcoholism, while others suffered from bouts of depression. In my decade and a half in journalism, I know of two who committed suicide." Lorch says war correspondents' job is to cover "the five D's": the Dead, the Dying, the Diseased, the Depressing, and the Dangerous.[3]

"In 3 years (in Africa)," Lorch wrote, "I reported on six civil wars, genocide, and massive refugee migrations. I walked over thousands of corpses. I was shot at, carjacked, arrested, and contracted cerebral malaria. It was a roller coaster of intense emotions, an adrenaline high that included raw fear and anger and horror and pure extreme fun. I loved it. I hated it."[4]

Many journalists are exhilarated when they confront danger and survive. "Some friends claim they are immune (from emotional distress)," Lorch wrote. "Many say they can't give up that thrill of being in war zones."[5] There is a tremendous emotional payoff in getting the story, getting it right, and telling the world. "The most important thing for me is 'Did I get the shot? Did I get it on tape?'" says Hoeffle. "What our life is all about is to record things and show the world and try to make a difference." Hoeffle repeatedly puts his life in danger to get the shot. Three cameramen died within yards of his position during the October revolt in Moscow in October 1993. "They were within yards of us," he said. "You say f——, that was really close. There were bullets sizzling through (but not hitting) our arms and legs."[6]

Like many reporters, Hoeffle takes great pride in his work. He considers it his duty to show the world what's going on. "It's one of the things that's so fantastic," he says. "To be able to capture what happens and show people. Hopefully, they'll see that it's so terrible that they have to stop making war."[7]

Lorch, who has been a reporter for *Newsweek, NBC News* and the *New York Times,* agrees. "I felt privileged to witness and write about history as it unfolded, to become part of people's lives and to make it real for others thousands of miles away," she wrote. "Sometimes I even felt I made a difference."[8]

Pride and satisfaction are only two of many emotions at work for reporters in war zones, however. There are others: horror, sadness, anger, irritability, fear, guilt, and many others. Far from immune to these emotions, reporters experience them at extremely high levels. They learn to compensate; they take care of each other. Sometimes they cry together after a bad day, telling their war stories long into the night. Sometimes they drink heavily. Some even take drugs.

Hoeffle's first war was in Cambodia in 1970. He and a group of CBS reporters barely escaped death at the hands of North Vietnamese soldiers. It was an experience he can recall vividly to this day: how the Vietnamese surrounded their car, how "we saw that they were going to shoot us," how he managed to speak German with one soldier who had studied in Communist East Berlin and convince him that the reporting team was German, not American, and should be released. "I was totally relaxed (as I talked to the North Vietnamese)," Hoeffle remembers. "I smiled. And then when I got back to the hotel in Phnom Penh, I collapsed and had a nervous breakdown. So we went out and toured (all the bars in) the town. That was the therapy. I went into a bar and said 'vodka.' He brought me a glass. I said 'no, I want the bottle.'"[9]

## REACTIONS TO TRAUMATIC STRESS

Distress is the most common reaction to a traumatic event, but there are many others: anger, irritability, fear, guilt, insomnia, difficulty in concentrating, sadness, tearfulness, and diminished appetite. For the vast majority of people, these reactions will dissipate over time. For some, however, debilitating responses will persist and develop into psychiatric disorders. Post-Traumatic Stress Disorder (PTSD) is perhaps the best known. As defined by the American Psychiatric Association's fourth edition of the *Diagnostic and Statistical Manual of Mental Disorders (DSM-IV)*,[10] PTSD is caused by being involved in or an eyewitness to a severe traumatic event that horrifies, terrifies, or renders one helpless.

While war correspondents are clearly at risk, a reporter does not have to go into a war zone to be exposed to traumatic stress. Crime, highway accidents, and natural disasters all are staples of print and broadcast media. Covering violence and death is the rule rather than the exception for many journalists. One preliminary study of journalists working for daily newspapers found that 86% of editors, reporters, and photographers had covered violent events "at the scene." Seventy-four percent (74%) had reported on fires, 66% on motor vehicle crashes, 56% on murders, 32% on air crashes, 29% on violent assaults, and 4% on earthquakes.[11] For reporters on the police beat, the experience is one of chronic exposure to violence. One crime reporter covered 216 stories on deaths and killings over a period of 11 months.[12] Traumatic exposure is also encountered in assignments such as sports writing and educational reporting.[13]

Reporters, whether they are on the police beat in small-town America or covering wars as a foreign correspondent, are often first-hand observers of violent death and other trauma. At times, journalists work in dangerous environments and are themselves at risk of harm.

When disaster strikes, journalists like Nick Spangler, who was a graduate student at Columbia University School of Journalism on September 11, 2001, react without assessing the risks. September 11 was primary election day in New York and Spangler was on a reporting assignment for one of his classes—following a city council candidate as he campaigned in lower Manhattan. Spangler heard a plane, "a heavy rasping sound," he wrote in *The Columbia Journalism Review*. He looked up and watched it crash into the World Trade Center. Like any reporter, Spangler ran toward the disaster, not away. His account is a litany of traumatic experience. "When we saw the bodies falling we were rendered inarticulate," Spangler wrote. They hit the ground with "a sound that, had I not seen the impact, I would have taken for an explosion." "I knew the body in front of me was a woman because she was wearing a skirt (sea-green)." "I saw a piece of somebody's leg get wrapped in burlap and left beneath a defoliated tree."[14]

Interviewed after his account was published in the *Columbia Journalism Review*, Spangler said he was well aware that "this was a huge, huge story." As he doggedly withstood danger all around in order to witness the disaster, Spangler "felt an intense passion in those hours, an exaltation. I felt alone at the center of the world." Not a rescuer, combatant, or victim, Spangler embraced his role as chronicler. "All details became iconic and crucial. I tried to record everything," he wrote.[15] But he also took note of a conflict reporters sometimes encounter when they cover such tragedies— the bigger the disaster, the bigger the story. The World Trade Center, with all its death and destruction was the story of a lifetime. Journalists are acutely aware that careers are made at such disasters. Of course, they are shocked and horrified by what they see. But are those feelings compounded by a sense of guilt?

"There is a girl who called me a vulture," Spangler wrote. "Vultures profit from disaster. When I ran to, and not from, the square, was I not on my way to exploiting this holocaust? Did I sense that the magnitude of the event could be made to magnify me? I cannot altogether refute this charge."[16]

When the first plane hit, Tom Flynn, a producer for *CBS News*, also made his way to the World Trade Center. "I got on my bike and headed straight down there. It never occurred to me to go the other way." Thinking like a reporter, a professional who covers news, Flynn was riding against a tide of people already streaming away from the disaster site. But he was determined to get there. "I knew this was a high-end story," he said. "This was the story of a lifetime. My one thought was that I could contribute (to how it was covered)."[17]

There are images from that day that Flynn will never forget: the people who jumped from the upper stories of the towers—"What were they thinking? What would motivate a person to do that? I've been thinking about that ever since." And saddest of all, there was a woman trying to get to the World Trade Center and a police officer who wouldn't let her into the danger zone. "She was on her knees screaming, 'Please! My daughter!' And he just kept saying 'Lady, you can't go back.' She didn't know it, but he was saving her life."[18]

Flynn barely survived when the first tower collapsed. "The guy next to me died. He disappeared. I saw him go under this huge chunk of building. I kept running." Riding his bike, he made it to the *CBS News* headquarters and immediately went on the air with Dan Rather. "As far as I know, it was the first eye witness report," Flynn said. "I was able to report the story faster and better than anybody. And I felt good about it, yes. Personally, I had set about reporting the story and I did it."[19]

Spangler and Flynn say they have vivid memories but are not haunted by the traumatic scenes they witnessed. "Not once have I been kept up at night," said Spangler.[20] Flynn says he feels no survivor guilt. "I would feel even more guilty if I had not survived. I have a daughter to take care of. I have things to do." Flynn did make changes in his life, however. "I went and bought a house on Cape Cod and put plans together for the rest of my life."[21] Spangler's report on what he saw at Ground Zero won him an internship at *The Miami Herald,* one he is sure he would not have gotten otherwise. His strongest emotion after the disaster was anger, but that has subsided. Both men have vivid memories of horrifying events, but those recollections are not intrusive. They sleep well and claim they do not have the other symptoms of PTSD: emotional numbing, a constriction of activities, impaired concentration, hyper-alertness, and a diminished sense of security.[22] Other journalists, however, have reported feelings of guilt. In the 2001 Freedom Forum panel, *Risking More than Their Lives* BBC's Allan Little noted, "What hit me like a sledgehammer was when I was working with somebody who was killed and I wasn't—I didn't know how to handle that at all. I thought it was my fault and was convinced everybody else thought it was my fault, and I wanted to swap places and be the one who was dead."[23]

There can also be guilt over the discrepancy between the standard of living of the journalists and those they cover. Janine di Giovanni, of the *New York Times,* described this reaction in response to Dr. Feinstein's research survey: "While I was answering Anthony's questionnaire, I had a very strong sense of guilt that I was being incredibly indulgent. If I had the ability to be tested for whether or not I had Post-Traumatic Stress Disorder, then I was privileged. The people who really needed it are my friends who've been raped, their villages burned, their possessions destroyed, the amputees I interviewed in Sierra Leone, the women in Kosovo who've been raped—yet they don't have this opportunity."[24]

Many people who survived the World Trade Center towers' collapse have suffered emotionally, but the intensity and severity of the traumatic stressors are not the sole determinants of who will develop psychiatric disorders. Individual factors such as a person's genetic makeup, physical and psychological state at the time of the event, coping style, past experience such as childhood abuse, and successful management of past challenges also play a role in determining the outcome.[25] Social supports, the recovery environment, and training and preparation also impact how a person responds. These factors are important to remember because they can be modified in order to prevent or limit disability.[26]

Reporters who frequent crime scenes and the battlefield build their own support system and coping mechanisms. They help each other, sharing their fear and sadness while they are in the battle zone. They often have great difficulty communicating their distress when they get home, however. "Telling your family just gets them scared," Hoeffle says. "They'll just worry about you."[27]

"Fear is an isolating experience," Lorch wrote, "one that is difficult to share. It is also an underestimated emotion. Most people experience fear in spurts, but what happens if you are constantly exposed to it day after day, night after night."[28]

Hoeffle, for one, is haunted by frequent nightmares. His bad dreams are always the same—there's a big news event right in front of him and he can't find a camera to record it. Once he dreamed that Martians had landed on Earth. It was an unbelievable scoop, the biggest story in the universe. But dream turned to nightmare as the anguished TV cameraman couldn't find the tool of his trade, the one thing that makes it worth all the risk and trauma—his camera.

Some photographers say their camera protects them from emotional distress. They cite what they call "viewfinder separation." "It's like you're watching it on TV, like it's not really happening," said Charlie Wilson, the *CBS News* cameraman who recorded the shooting of President Ronald Reagan and three others in 1981. "It was only later that I realized people were being shot all around me."[29]

Other photographers report that their work intensifies distress. As Steve Northup, a photographer whose work has appeared in top publications all over the world, said, "As painful as it is to view, this kind of work is even more difficult to produce. We, the viewer see only a tiny slice of time. The photographer sees it all, hears it all, smells it all, and can't hide behind the camera. When you are photographing terrible things you have to pay extra attention. You become one with the scene; the camera almost disappears."[30] Given this intense exposure to trauma, researchers and journalists have posited that photojournalists would be at greater risk to develop PTSD. This prediction, however, has not been borne out by research. Two recent studies found that photographers were not more likely to develop PTSD.[31]

War correspondents, on the other hand, have been noted to have higher rates of illness. Anthony Feinstein conducted a study of 140 seasoned reporters who had spent an average of 15 years in war zones and a comparison group of Canadian journalists who had never gone off to war.[32] Feinstein found that 20 percent of war correspondents met criteria for "probable PTSD" (three times higher than the control group) and that one-third were classified as "psychologically distressed."[33]

Certain types of traumas are more likely to result in PTSD than others. Intentional violence such as torture, rape, and assault produces the highest rates. The 1995 bombing of the Murrah building in Oklahoma City, for example, was associated with PTSD in 35% of those directly exposed to the attack.[34] In general, the greater the degree of traumatic exposure, the greater the risk of developing subsequent psychiatric illness. Elements of the traumatic event that increase the intensity of psychological and physiological responses include the perceived threat, degree of controllability and predictability; the efficacy of attempts to minimize injuries to oneself and others; exposure to heat, cold, or pain; actual injury or loss; and noxious smells, surprise, and darkness.[35]

Five to six percent of American men and 10–14% of American women are estimated to have had PTSD at some point in their lives, making PTSD the fourth most common psychiatric disorder in the United States.[36] Stressors that are severe enough to be considered traumatic include: combat, sexual assault, muggings, serious car crashes, witnessing death or injury, and learning about traumas to others.

Other psychiatric conditions such as major depression can develop following traumatic stress. An individual may develop more than one diagnosis. For example, PTSD and depression are often found together. Symptoms of depression include insomnia, an increase or decrease in appetite, concentration difficulties, tearfulness or irritability, loss of interest and pleasure in sex and other activities, feelings of guilt, diminished energy, and thoughts that one would be better off dead. Traumatic bereavement, increased use of alcohol and cigarettes, and family violence also increase following exposure to catastrophic events.[37] Some people experience physical symptoms that they may or may not recognize as connected to the traumatic exposure. Frequently, these individuals will go to their primary care provider with complaints of shortness of breath, palpitations, unexplained pain, insomnia, nausea, and mood swings.[38] Psychological factors can contribute to medical illness—from heart disease[39] to diabetes.[40]

In addition to primary traumatic stressors such as exposure to the dead, there are secondary stressors, factors stemming from the event that also influence psychological outcomes. The individual's recovery environment plays an important role in determining an event's meaning and creating a sense of physical and emotional security. For example, journalists who reside in an area that is directly impacted by a disaster or war generally have a much different experience than those who are from outside the community. The normal stressors encountered in covering a horrific event are magnified by the disruption of one's own sense of security and predictability and by familiarity with victims and responders. Local reporters covering a hurricane may have to cope with damage to their own homes even as they must work overtime to cover the story. The stressors multiply: home repairs, alternate childcare arrangements, a multitude of other energy-consuming activities just when the workload is at its peak. Secondary stressors that result from catastrophes, for example, relocation, job loss, fighting with insurance companies, and loss of social supports, can cause additional distress and may themselves contribute to psychiatric illness.

Increasing attention is being paid to better understanding factors related to resiliency. For example, what protected the 65% who did not develop PTSD following the Oklahoma City bombing? For some, a traumatic experience can facilitate positive changes. It can prompt a re-evaluation of priorities and values and provide a clearer direction and sense of purpose.

## JOURNALISTS AND TRAUMA

### Prevention Strategies

#### Training and Education

Training can diminish adverse psychological outcomes from traumatic exposure in a number of ways. It can help journalists limit or alter their exposure, decrease unexpectedness and surprise, and promote a sense of mastery and hope. In interviews with survivors of a helicopter crash, Hytten examined what elements of training had been most helpful.[41] The largest advantage noted was that the training allowed the survivors to remain calm and pursue alternate escape routes when the initial ones were blocked. Training also afforded confidence that the situation could be survived because of prior success under simulated conditions.[42]

Journalists in consultation with former soldiers developed the Hostile Environments Training Course. It emphasizes heightened awareness of hidden dangers and risk assessment, using this awareness to minimize danger. The course addresses physical and psychological survival in extreme climates, personal security, how to identify mob danger signs, and other topics. It includes experiential as well as classroom learning. Yannis Behrakis, the Reuters photographer who escaped an ambush in Sierra Leone that took the lives of two colleagues, credits the course with his survival.[43] Other journalists have reported that the course has allowed them to successfully navigate land mines and to use first-aid training to help an injured colleague.[44] Thought should be given to developing other training to teach journalists how to remain safe in the face of more commonly experienced dangers or to incorporate this into undergraduate journalism.

Journalists are now confronted with the possibility of covering stories on terrorist events in which biological, chemical, nuclear, or radiological agents are used. It is incumbent upon news organizations to provide journalists with protective equipment and realistic training using the gear; to modify a military expression, "train the way you report." Studies of individuals involved in chemical/biological warfare (CBW) training have shown that 10–20% of participants experienced moderate to severe psychological symptoms including claustrophobia, anxiety, and panic.[45] The exercises were ended prematurely by 4–8% of the participants, who experienced hyperventilation, psychophysiological complaints, visual and time distortion, shaking, tremors, claustrophobia, and a desire to flee. Working in personal protective equipment increases exertion especially in hot weather, and wearers must learn how to drink safely in order to prevent dehydration and exhaustion.

Education on traumatic stress is important. It diminishes the sense of going crazy in those who begin to experience distressing responses. Learning strategies for limiting traumatic exposure, for example, avoiding looking at the faces and hands of the dead, thereby, reducing identification (the sense of "that could be my child") can be beneficial. Education may reduce stigma and encourage journalists to reach out to colleagues. Importantly, it can lead to early recognition and treatment of those journalists who are having problems, hopefully, interrupting a downward spiral of increasing isolation and suffering.

Other professional groups that go on assignments entailing exposure to death and destruction have incorporated education programs to assist professionals and their families with reintegration following deployments. The military, for example, has developed extensive materials and training to facilitate return.

### Experience

Experience seems to be something of a double-edged sword in coping with traumatic events. Exposure to violence and destruction can lead to a better ability to handle future events ("inoculation") or can lead to sensitization and increased vulnerability. Studies of combat soldiers and humanitarian aid workers suggest that the relationship between psychological distress and trauma experience is a u-shaped curve: high distress in the inexperienced upon first exposure, which decreases with experience, but then climbs again at some point when one has seen too much. The photographer James Nachtwey describes sensitization: "I've probably seen thousands of dead people, and it does not get any easier. It gets more difficult. You become more sensitized, not less sensitized. Suffering gets more difficult to witness."[46]

Often young reporters eager to establish themselves seek out difficult assignments as quickly as possible. Horst Faas talked about the value of getting experience before going into a war zone: "When I go through our *Requiem* book (a book of photographs by photographers killed in Vietnam), I see that about half of them were so inexperienced they shouldn't have been there. But they were ambitious and wanted to make the headlines; some did, but only when they got killed. There were so many that walked into my office in Saigon that had never been anywhere." Gradual exposure to difficult stories, analogous to the gradual introduction of medical students to illness and death during their training, may bolster coping skills. Faas encourages reporters to cut their teeth on challenging but less dangerous assignments before becoming war correspondents: "Today I try and talk people out of going to these zones. I say: 'Do Northern Ireland first. Do foot-and-mouth disease.'"[47]

More commonly, new journalists are sent to accident scenes or to interview family members after fatalities. Simpson and Boggs asked journalists how prepared they had been for what they experienced on their first trauma assignment. Forty-six percent said they were not at all prepared while another 26% reported that they were not well prepared; only 28% felt that they were adequately or well prepared.[48] Pairing novices with more experienced workers has been reported to reduce distress in a variety of other professions dealing with trauma and disasters and may also help journalists.

### Organizational leadership

Leaders such as editors, producers, publishers, and network executives can help prevent traumatic stress or they can exacerbate it. There is an inherent tension between the need to make profits often requiring more intense coverage of violent scenes and journalists' emotional and physical well-being. For example, some news organizations have made decisions to forego stories in order to protect their journalists from entering dangerous areas, thereby letting the competition scoop them. At the other end of the spectrum are organizations that provide no training, little protective equipment, and send inexperienced journalists in harm's way. Freelancers, having no organizational support, are viewed by many as the most vulnerable to physical and psychological injury.

Some media organizations have developed policies and practices that have proved helpful in dealing with traumatic stress and the ordinary strain of reporting. Making time for staff to talk about their traumatic stories, giving clear feedback from editors to the staff about how well they're doing their job, providing counselors, giving more time off, rotating staff assignments, and recognizing that reporters have limits are lessons learned by one managing editor.[49] Elizabeth Neuffer covered Bosnia for

*The Boston Globe*, "My editors were always concerned for my safety, and never wished me to take unnecessary risks to get a story, and for that they deserve great credit. Not all editors were so wise. But we never talked about Bosnia's legacy, about how I walked out of that newsroom to go to Bosnia as one woman, and returned to it as someone else. We never spoke about how guilty I felt for not having done more, about how responsible I still feel for the people I know there, for how much I wished I had more power to change events than just that of my pen. We never talked about the fact that Bosnia will always haunt me—in both positive and negative ways."[50]

As noted above, providing training and education are important preventive steps. Good health insurance plans that include coverage for mental health treatment should be offered as part of the benefits package for journalists. In the event of the death of a journalist, "grief leadership,"[51] expressing sadness and loss rather than stoicism, can encourage the expression of shared grief to emphasize the normality of and necessity of grieving.

Leaders can be vigilant for journalists who appear to be struggling. Journalists have described outward symptoms of stress in colleagues: hostility, anger, depression, headaches, stomach problems, crying, excessive smoking and drinking, cynicism, repetitious stories about the event, overly loud speech, and mood swings.[52] Allan Little described getting into treatment: "I'd heard of Post-Traumatic Stress Disorder, but thought it was an indulgent, nancy-boy thing. It was a terrible experience, and I became very moody and paranoid, socially dysfunctional and unable to work, and it was to do with being alive. The only way I could get out of it was to go and get help. This was about nine years ago. It wasn't voluntary—I thought I was fine. It was one of my bosses—significantly, a woman—who said to me: 'you look like shit. You're in a state, and I've made an appointment for you to go and see somebody.'"[53]

## Coping Strategies

The process of journal writing has long been recognized to be helpful in recovering from painful events. Many reporters find that the process of writing down their experiences helps them integrate the horror they have seen. Janine di Giovanni, of the *New York Times*, noted: "I am a writer and, therefore, feel that I am able to cleanse myself, that I can write and film my story and that a lot of the trauma I've seen comes out in my writing and then it's over with."[54]

Talking with colleagues and friends is also an important part of working through a traumatic event. Seeking out someone who is empathic, trustworthy, and who has faced similar difficulties can be an important step in weaving the trauma into the fabric of one's history rather than having it as a disjointed, painful event that takes on a life of its own.

Di Giovanni describes the value of friendship at painful times: "This current generation of war correspondents has been together for a long time. Some of us are very close, some aren't. It tends to give a sense of family, you know the people you're with. This came to light when Kurt Schork and Miguel Gil were killed. Being able to have that solidarity and to talk to people has certainly helped me. I've never been treated for post-traumatic stress. I've just always had sympathetic friends who listen to me."[55]

Talking about experiences with people who do not share a similar context can create awkwardness and be more isolating. Allan Little discussed the experience of a friend of his who had spent two years in Burundi and Rwanda: "He took some time off and flew back to London and was having dinner at his brother's, at a conventional London dinner party. Just before the food was served, his brother's five-year-old child came to kiss his parents good night. When the child left the room, my friend said, 'That's the first live child I've seen in a year.' And, of course, it ruined the entire evening."[56]

The value of talking through events is reflected in the popularity of debriefing. Many news organizations now bring in mental health experts to conduct debriefings after critical incidents. There is considerable debate in the scientific literature on the efficacy of debriefing, and there are some instances in which debriefing has been thought to be harmful.[57] Therefore, there is now consensus among leading researchers in the field that it is unethical to make debriefings mandatory.[58] In this regard, Frank Ochberg articulated an excellent guiding principle for assisting journalists following exposure to trauma: "The philosophy will be not to stigmatize or psychiatrise the process of talking about trauma, but to find ways of having it occur that are appropriate for the culture and the climate of the organization in which this occurs."[59]

### Journalists and Trauma: The Dart Foundation

Well before journalism and trauma became formally linked, Michigan-based psychiatrist Frank Ochberg had a vision: To create something that would benefit both journalists who covered traumatic events and the victims they wrote about. His experience to tackle this mission came with the unique perspective of knowing mental health professionals, victims affected by the media and, eventually, the journalists who dealt with them.

Now the concept has gone far beyond this simple idea, reaching into countries as diverse as Australia and Rwanda and influencing everyone from hard-core war correspondents to those who cover the daily police beat.

"We are a wonderful species, but also a deplorable species, contaminated by cruelty, indifference, intolerance, arrogance and hypocrisy,"

Ochberg wrote. "Dart Center was created by kindred spirits in journalism and the mental health profession to explore the interface of these fields, and thereby enlighten and assist humanity in its internal (perhaps eternal) conflict."

Ochberg's early ideas were vague and fluid, but some things stood firm: The Dart Center would induce change rather than simply toe the line. It would stay flexible. And it would equip journalists with what they needed to interview victims without retraumatizing them.

At the same time, the Center gradually realized the toll that covering traumatic events took on journalists and vowed to ensure their care while doing their job. This had to be done carefully and diligently, with a light touch from professionals and a strong bond among the journalists themselves.

Ochberg, known affectionately as the Center's "indigenous rabbi," has deliberately pulled the reins on his group, keeping growth slow and guiding it with a fatherly hand. Each new element is carefully considered and honed, while the agenda flows with the times and takes the pace that journalists need.

The Center is named after the family of William Dart, of Mason, Michigan, who has been its primary funder. Until then, no one had truly connected journalism and trauma and its effects on both sides. The Dart Center began at Michigan State University, which provided Ochberg with an adjunct Professor of Journalism role and embraced the topic of journalism and trauma in the early 1990s. MSU also hosted the first Dart award.

To attract attention early on, the Dart Center offered an annual $10,000 prize for the newspaper entry that best covered victims with sensitivity and complexity. Judges included not only journalists and editors but a victim advocate and someone in the psychological field. The Dart Award has expanded into an Australian version as well and is believed to be the only one of its kind today. It is also supported by the International Society for Traumatic Stress Studies (ISTSS), a strong Dart link.

Four years ago, Dart began awarding a Fellowship program to six mid-career journalists for a weeklong retreat in plush surroundings while professionals educated them on traumatic stress. The Fellowship is timed with the annual convention for the ISTSS, giving journalists a chance to attend seminars and hear from carefully selected academic leaders about the clinical side of trauma. The real bonus comes when the Fellows inevitably open up to one another, thus, forging what may well become lifelong friendships and a network of self-help therapists.

This year, a Web-based meeting place known as the Dart Society is taking root, where Dart Fellows and some selected award winners find refuge in discussing the day's dilemmas. This was particularly useful when the *Wall Street Journal* reporter Daniel Pearl was gruesomely killed. For some of these already traumatized journalists, the first place they turned to was to each other, via the Dart Society.

Creativity continued when, after September 11, the Dart Center temporarily funded Dart Center–Ground Zero (DCGZ), a New York City–based enterprise designed to help journalists affected by covering the attacks. Ground Zero's two directors, Elana Newman, a University of Tulsa psychology professor, and Barb Monseu, a former Jefferson County public school administrator who handled the Columbine tragedy, have gone into full alert to help journalists while documenting the results. David Handschuh, a *New York Post* photojournalist, injured while covering the tragedy, has joined DCGZ to help plan outreach projects and seminars.

The Dart Center also looks forward to a new generation of journalists with liaisons created with several universities. The University of Washington has its own Center for Journalism and Trauma and operates the Dart Center, and the University of Central Oklahoma, University of Indiana and Purdue University–Indianapolis, University of Colorado, and Queensland University of Technology in Australia have adopted similar programs.

Some newsrooms have also responded. CNN International, the British Broadcasting Corporation and other organizations have asked the Dart Center for advice and support, especially in the wake of the September 11 tragedy. Before that, the *Daily Oklahoman* began a policy of providing counseling for reporters after the Oklahoma City bombing that paid dividends when the same journalists covered the May 3, 1999, tornadoes that killed 42 people.

Brave articles published in the *Society of Professional Journalist's Quill* magazine, the *Washington Post,* and elsewhere have thrown open the doors to the truth of trauma, finally allowing journalists to balk at the machoism that comes from claiming to remain unaffected.

Eloquent breakthrough pieces have come from Indiana University Professor Sherry Ricchiardi, who has reported on journalism and trauma in the *American Journalism Review,* both domestically and abroad.

Frank Smyth, a freelance journalist and head of the Washington, D.C.–based Committee to Protect Journalists, revealed his anguish publicly after having it fester since he was held captive by Iraqis in Desert Storm a decade ago. That was quite a feat, considering he only recently spoke of it privately with other Dart participants. "It took me years to be able to even really talk about the experience, let alone write about it," wrote Smyth in the March 2002 edition of *Quill* magazine. "The kicker is obvious. Everyone is responsible for their own actions, and each of us is defined in life by every choice we make."[60]

The choices the Dart Center makes will continue to affect journalists in many ways. Rwandans met two Dart fellows last year who have since written about their plight and asked for money to buy computers for their journalism school. Soon, another Dart contingency will travel to South Africa for a similar venture.

Simply put, the Dart Center has attempted to humanize the culture of covering traumatic situations. Like it or not, journalists are relenting to the idea that they, as well as their sources, may be victims of PTSD, or of merely needing someone to talk with after a rough assignment.

The fact that the Dart Center is expanding into areas such as Rwanda, Africa, Europe, and Asia shows that American journalists are not unique in the effects their careers have on them. In fact, the need may be stronger in more unstable regions with less governmental support.

Dart recognizes the need and puts forth the effort.

## CONCLUSIONS

Journalists witness trauma and violence routinely in the course of reporting on the news. The bigger and more dangerous the story, the greater the personal and professional payoff. As Nicholas Kristof summarized one assignment: "In one stint covering the Congo civil war, I was in a plane crash, was chased through the jungle for two days by rebel guerrillas and caught the most lethal form of malaria. Yet the rewards of digging up tough, fresh stories made it perhaps the most satisfying trip I've ever made."

Yet with the satisfaction of bearing witness, the exhilaration of making deadlines, and the camaraderie, there also comes the emotional toll of witnessing suffering and cruelty and, sometimes, losing friends. Talking with fellow journalists or writing down the narrative can help to validate and place the events in a context. Usually, transient reactions dissipate and a new equilibrium is established. At times, however, the disquieting feelings and thoughts do not go away and the past continues to intrude into the present. The increased use of alcohol to numb the pain, increased risk taking, social isolation, and other actions can lead to increased suffering and professional and interpersonal problems. The early recognition of persistent psychiatric symptoms and timely intervention can interrupt this negative cycle and help prevent chronic psychiatric disorders. Increased appreciation of the psychiatric consequences of trauma can lead to individual and organizational efforts in prevention and early intervention.

## EPILOGUE: EDITORS AND STRESS

Stress arises not only from reporters who are called upon to witness horrific acts but also editors who somehow must sift everyday through all the material presented from the field and try to figure out which is worthy of coverage, whether it is fair and balanced, whether it may breach national security, whether the stories will incite libel suits up ahead, and many other important questions. In the 1980s the Associated Press Managing Editors organization conducted the second of two newspaper industry surveys of editors and stress. The results were reported to editors attending the 1983 APME National Convention in Louisville, Kentucky. In discussing the effects of stress on American newspaper editors, the following was discovered:[61]

- The effects of stress can cover a broad range from excitement, satisfaction, and challenge, to frustration, distress, and illness. Most editors feel their environment at work is not supportive, their vulnerability is high, and that stressors occur frequently and are felt intensely.
- These are the editors who Dr. Paul Rosch of the American Institute of Stress said are likely to have health problems as a result.
- In fact, 39 percent of the editors responding, or 212, said they have had or were now experiencing a health problem related to stress on the job.
- Some 33 percent said they have experienced health problems from a list that included ulcers, asthma, hypertension, cancer, heart disease, arthritis, stroke, alcoholism, or drug abuse.
- The number of editors reporting stress-related health problems increased from the first APME study.
- The situations editors say cause them negative stress are the types of situations scientists have tied to illness.
- These situations fall into two categories for editors: those in which editors say they no longer have the control they had, or believe they should have, and situations in which they cannot take pride in what they are doing.
- The survey does not suggest that being an editor is more stressful than being an executive in another profession. But the researchers did conclude that at least some of the stressors at work on editors are those that can definitely lead to health problems.
- Stress is different for each individual, and a person's vulnerability to it depends on how each editor feels about the job.
- It is apparent that not everyone who operates under intense pressure or unrelieved stress becomes ill. Many individuals flourish under stress and, if they have control, they are highly productive and enjoy the challenge.

Comments from some of the responding editors themselves were revealing and included the following:

- "I have gone through 19 years as a managing editor and editor having had a heart attack. If you can do that, you can cope with stress. The individual creates stress—not the situation."
- "I have been in this business 30 years. I don't think I could function apart from a daily deadline. I find the newspaper business stimulating. For the most part I love it, but after finishing this survey I wonder why I'm not a basket case."

- "My observations are based on past stress experiences, which ruined my marriage, created heavy drinking and weight and mental/emotional problems. I have since conquered stress, and can cope with the daily problems it creates. I have also become expert in observing it in my staff, and dealing with their stress problems as they occur."

Robert Giles, then editor of the *Rochester Democrat-Gazette* in New York, presented the report and noted:

For years we have accepted the idea that stress is part of the newspaper life. It is, but not in the ways that we imagined. The adrenaline that flows when we are on deadline or in the grip of a big story works like an injection, giving us a burst of energy to focus on the day's news. That stress is what we love about newspapers— the editor role, directing the staff and shaping the newspaper. The adrenaline also flows when we confront the frustrations of the manager role, when duty compels us to act for the company in ways that seem to be not in the best interest of readers. That stress bores into our pride and strips us of the sense that we are in control. It can leave us dispirited and vulnerable.[62]

## NOTES

1. K. Hoeffle and M. E. Walsh, conversation, 25 February 2002.

2. D. Lorch, "Surviving the Five Ds," *Media Studies Journal* (summer 2001): 98–103.

3. Ibid.

4. Ibid.

5. Ibid.

6. Hoeffle and Walsh, conversation, 25 February 2002.

7. Ibid.

8. Lorch, "Surviving the Five Ds," 98–103.

9. Hoeffle and Walsh, conversation, 25 February 2002.

10. American Psychiatric Association, *Diagnostic and Statistical Manual of Mental Disorders*, 4th ed. (Washington, D.C.: American Psychiatric Association, 1994).

11. R. A. Simpson and J. G. Boggs, "An Exploratory Study of Traumatic Stress among Newspaper Journalists," *Journalism and Communication Monographs* 1 (1999): 1–26.

12. R. A. Simpson, "Swimming a 'Wild, Raging River,'" *Nieman Reports* (fall 1996): 33–34.

13. J. Maxson, "Training Journalism Students to Deal with Trauma," *Journalism and Mass Communication Educator* (Spring 2000): 79–86; and B. Dwyre, "The Test of a Sportswriter," *Nieman Reports* (Fall 1996): 19–20.

14. N. Spangler, "Witness," *Columbia Journalism Review* (November/December 2001): 6–9.

15. Ibid.

16. Ibid.

17. T. Flynn and M. E. Walsh, conversation, 28 February 2002.

18. Ibid.

19. Ibid.

20. Spangler, "Witness," 6–9.

21. T. Flynn and M. E. Walsh, conversation, 28 February 2002.

22. F. Ochberg, "A Primer on Covering Victims," *Nieman Reports* (fall 1996): 21–26.

23. J. Owen et al., *Risking More Than Their Lives: The Effects of Post-Traumatic Stress Disorder on Journalists* (New York: Freedom Forum European Centre: Freedom Forum, First Amendment Center, 2001).

24. Ibid.

25. Ochberg, "A Primer on Covering Victims," 21–26; and B. Raphael and R. J. Ursano, "Psychological Debriefing," in *Sharing the Front Line and the Back Hills: Peacekeepers, Humanitarian Aid Workers and the Media in the Midst of Crisis,* ed. Y. Danieli (Amityville, N.Y.: Baywood Publishing Company, 2002), 343–352.

26. Raphael and Ursano, "Psychological Debriefing," 343–352.

27. Hoeffle and Walsh, conversation, 25 February 2002.

28. Lorch, "Surviving the Five Ds," 98–103.

29. C. Wilson and M. E. Walsh, personal conversation, 5 February 2002.

30. S. Northup, "Photographers Can't Hide Behind Their Cameras," *Nieman Reports* 54, no. 3 (2000): 49–51.

31. E. Newman, "The Bridge between Sorrow and Knowledge: Journalists and Traumatic Stress," in *Sharing the Front Line and the Back Hills: Peacekeepers, Humanitarian Aid Workers and the Media in the Midst of Crisis,* ed. Y. Danieli (Amityville, N.Y.: Baywood Publishing Company, 2002), 316–322.

32. J. Owen, *Risking More Than Their Lives;* and A. Feinstein and J. Owen, "Journalists, War and Post-Traumatic Stress Disorder," in *Sharing the Front Line and the Back Hills: Peacekeepers, Humanitarian Aid Workers and the Media in the Midst of Crisis,* ed. Y. Danieli (Amityville, N.Y.: Baywood Publishing Company), 305–315.

33. Feinstein and Owen, "Journalists, War and Post-Traumatic Stress Disorder," 305–315.

34. C. S. North, Nixon, and S. E. A. Shariate, "Psychiatric Disorders among Survivors of the Oklahoma City Bombing," *Journal of the American Medical Association* 282 (1999): 755–762.

35. R. Yehuda, "Post-Traumatic Stress Disorder," *New England Journal of Medicine,* 346, no. 2 (2002): 108–114; and R. J. Ursano, C. S. Fullerton, and A. E. Norwood, "Psychiatric Dimensions of Disaster: Patient Care, Community Consultation, and Preventive Medicine, *Harvard Review of Psychiatry* 3, no. 4 (1995): 196–209.

36. Yehuda, "Post-Traumatic Stress Disorder," 108–114.

37. Ursano, Fullerton, and Norwood, "Psychiatric Dimensions of Disaster," 196–209.

38. Yehuda, "Post-Traumatic Stress Disorder," 108–114.

39. J. Leor, W. K. Poole, and R. A. Kloner, "Sudden Cardiac Death Triggered by an Earthquake," *New England Journal of Medicine* 334 (1996): 413–419.

40. A. Jacobson, "The Psychological Care of Patients with Insulin-Dependent Diabetes Mellitus," *New England Journal of Medicine* 334 (1996): 1249–1253.

41. K. Hytten, "Helicopter Crash in Water: Effects of Simulator Escape Training," *Acta Psychiatrica Scandinavica,* 80, suppl. 355 (1989): 50–55.

42. R. J. Ursano, T. A. Grieger, and J. E. McCarroll, "Prevention of Post-traumatic Stress: Consultation, Training and Early Treatment," in *Traumatic Stress: The Effects*

*of Overwhelming Experience on Mind, Body and Society,* ed. B .A. van der Kolk, A.C. McFarlane, and L. Weisaeth(Guilford, N.Y.: Guilford Press, 1996), 441–462.

43. B. Mills, P. Rees, and G.J. Turnbull, "Centurion: Shielding Journalists and Aid Workers," in *Sharing the Front Line and the Back Hills: Peacekeepers, Humanitarian Aid Workers and the Media in the Midst of Crisis,* ed. Y. Danieli (Amityville, N.Y.: Baywood Publishing Company, 2002), 323–330.

44. J. Owen, P. Rees, and J. Seward, "Journalists Learn How to Protect Themselves in War," *Nieman Reports* (fall 2000): 59–60.

45. C.S. Fullerton and R.J. Ursano, "Behavioral and Psychological Responses to Chemical and Biological Warfare," *Military Medicine* 155, no. 2 (1990): 54–59.

46. B. Staples, "The Perils of Growing Comfortable with Evil," *Nieman Reports* (fall 2000): 52–53.

47. J. Owen, *Risking More Than Their Lives.*

48. Simpson and Boggs, "An Exploratory Study of Traumatic Stress among Newspaper Journalists," 1–26.

49. Simpson, "Swimming a 'Wild, Raging River,'" 33–34.

50. E. Neuffer, "A Piece of Our Soul," in *Sharing the Front Lines and The Back Hills : Peacekeepers, Humanitarian Aid Workers and the Media in the Midst of Crisis,* ed. Y. Danieli (Amityville, N.Y.: Baywood Publishing Company, 2002), 286–287.

51. L.H. Ingraham, "Grief Leadership," in *The Human Response to the Gander Military Air Disaster: A Summary Report,* ed. K. Wright (Washington, D.C.: Walter Reed Army Institute of Research, 1987), 10–13.

52. Simpson and Boggs, "An Exploratory Study of Traumatic Stress among Newspaper Journalists," 1–26.

53. J. Owen, *Risking More Than Their Lives.*

54. Ibid.

55. Ibid.

56. Ibid.

57. Raphael and Ursano, "Psychological Debriefing," 343–352.

58. U.S. Department of Defense, U.S. Department of Health and Human Services, The National Institute of Mental Health, The Substance Abuse and Mental Health Services Administration, Center for Mental Health Services, U.S. Department of Justice, Office for Victims of Crime, U.S. Department of Veterans Affairs, National Center for PTSD, and The American Red Cross, "Mental Health and Mass Violence—Evidence Based on Early Psychological Intervention for Victims/ Survivors of Mass Violence: A Workshop to Reach Consensus on Best Practices" (workshop at Aerlie Conference Center, Warrenton, Va., 2000).

59. J. Owen, *Risking More Than Their Lives.*

60. F. Smyth, "Caught in an Unfriendly Land," *Quill Magazine* 90, no. 2 (2002): 34–35.

61. Robert H. Giles, *Editors and Stress: A Report to APME on Stress and How It Affects the Lives of Newspaper Editors,* Continuing Studies Committee, Associated Press Managing Editors, Louisville, Kentucky, 1–4 November 1983.

62. Ibid.

# Selected Bibliography

Adam, G. Stuart, *Toward a Definition of Journalism: Understanding an Old Craft as an Art Form.* The Poynter Papers, no. 2. St. Petersburg: Poynter Institute for Media Studies, 1992.

Barlett, Donald L., and James B. Steele. *America: What Went Wrong?* Kansas City: Andrews and McMeel, 1992.

Berry, Thomas Elliott. *Journalism in America.* New York: Hastings House, 1976.

Bragg, Rick. *Somebody Told Me.* Tuscaloosa: University of Alabama Press, 2000.

Clark, Roy Peter. *The American Conversation and the Language of Journalism.* The Poynter Papers, no. 5. St. Petersburg: Poynter Institute for Media Studies, 1993.

Epstein, Edward Jay. *News from Nowhere: Television and the News.* New York: Vintage Books, 1974.

Fitzhenry, Robert I, ed. *The Harper Book of Quotations,* 3d ed. New York: Harper-Collins, 1995.

Fuller, Jack. *News Values: Ideas for an Information Age.* Chicago: University of Chicago Press, 1996.

Gans, Herbert J. *Deciding What's News.* New York: Vintage Books, 1980.

Goleman, Daniel. *Emotional Intelligence: Why It Can Matter More Than I.Q.* New York: Bantam, 1995.

Harrington, Walt. *Intimate Journalism: The Art and Craft of Reporting Everyday Life.* Thousand Oaks, Calif.: Sage, 1997.

Hausman, Carl. *The Decision-Making Process in Journalism.* Chicago: Nelson-Hall, 1987.

Hayakawa, S. I. *Language in Thought and Action,* 4th ed. New York: Harcourt, Brace, Jovanovich, 1978.

Keir, Gerry, Maxwell McCombs, and Donald L. Shaw. *Advanced Reporting: Beyond News Events.* Prospect Heights, Ill.: Waveland Press, 1991.

Kessler, Lauren. *The Dissident Press*. Thousand Oaks: Sage, 1984.

Liebling, A. J. *The Press*. New York: Pantheon, 1961.

Lippmann, Walter, *Public Opinion*. New York: Macmillan, 1922.

Malcolm, Janet. *The Journalist and the Murderer*. New York: Vintage Books, 1990.

McDougall, Curtis. *Interpretive Reporting*, 4th ed. New York: Macmillan, 1963.

Merrill, John C. *The Imperative of Freedom: A Philosophy of Journalistic Autonomy*. New York: Hastings House, 1980.

Meyer, Philip. *The New Precision Journalism*. Bloomington: Indiana University Press, 1991.

Mindich, David T. Z. *Just the Facts: How "Objectivity" Came to Define American Journalism*. New York: New York University Press, 1998.

Mott, Frank Luther. *American Journalism*, 3d ed. New York: Macmillan, 1962.

Rivers, William. *Finding Facts: Interviewing, Observing, Using Reference Sources*. Englewood Cliffs, N.J.: Prentice-Hall, 1975.

Schudson, Michael. *Discovering the News: A Social History of News in the United States*. New York: Basic Books, 1978.

Snyder, Louis L., and Richard B. Morris, eds. *A Treasury of Great Reporting*. New York: Simon and Schuster, 1961.

vanGinneken, Jaap. *Understanding Global News: A Critical Introduction*. Thousand Oaks: Sage, 1998.

Willis, Jim and Albert Adelowo Okunade. *Reporting on Risks: The Practice and Ethics of Health and Safety Communication*. Westport, Conn: Praeger, 1997.

Willis, Jim. *The Shadow World: Life Between the News Media and Reality*. Westport, Conn.: Praeger, 1991.

Willis, Jim. *Journalism: State of the Art*. Westport: Praeger, 1990.

Wolfe, Tom. *The New Journalism*. New York: Harper and Row, 1963.

# Index

## About the Author

JIM WILLIS holds the Chair of the Communication Studies Department at Azusa Pacific University. Prior to that he held the Hardin Chair of Excellence in Journalism at the University of Memphis. He is a veteran of more than a decade in the news business and two decades in the university classroom teaching journalism. He is a former reporter and editor with *The Daily Oklahoman* and *The Dallas Morning News*. He has authored or coauthored seven books on journalism and the news media and he continues to report on significant events for newspapers such as *The Daily Oklahoman*.